The Excel Edge – Mastering Spreadsheets for Business and Beyond

In this book

Chapter 1: Getting Started with Excel - 13

- Introduction to Excel and its interface - 14
- Creating and saving a new workbook - 17
- Formatting options - 19
- Entering and editing data - 21

Chapter 2: Working with Formulas and Functions – 24

- Understanding basic arithmetic operators - 25
- Writing simple formulas - 28
- Introduction to functions - 30
- Using absolute and relative cell references - 37

Chapter 3: Managing Worksheets and Workbooks - 40

- Renaming, moving, and deleting worksheets - 41
- Creating and managing workbooks - 43
- Protecting and unprotecting worksheets and workbooks - 46
- Using the Page Layout and Print options - 49

Chapter 4: Formatting and Presenting Data - 52

- Formatting cells for dates, numbers, and text - 53
- Using Conditional Formatting to highlight data - 56
- Creating and formatting tables - 60
- Adding charts and graphs to visualize data - 64

Chapter 5: Advanced Formulas and Functions - 68

- Advanced functions - 69
- Using nested functions - 72
- Working with arrays and array formulas - 74
- Using logical functions like AND, OR, and NOT - 77

Chapter 6: Working with PivotTables -80

- Understanding PivotTables and their benefits - 81
- Creating PivotTables from data - 84
- Sorting, filtering, and grouping data in PivotTables - 86
- Using PivotCharts to visualize PivotTable data - 89

Chapter 7: Using Macros for Automation - 93

- Understanding macros and their benefits - 94
- Creating and running simple macros - 97
- Assigning macros to buttons and keyboard shortcuts - 100
- Editing and deleting macros - 103

Chapter 8: Collaborating and Sharing Workbooks - 106

- Sharing workbooks with others - 107
- Protecting and sharing specific cells or ranges - 109
- Using comments and track changes to collaborate - 113
- Importing and exporting data from other sources - 115

Chapter 9: Tips and Tricks for Excel - 118

- Keyboard shortcuts to save time - 119
- Using templates and add-ins - 121
- Troubleshooting common issues in Excel - 141
- Best practices for organizing and managing data - 144

Chapter 10: Excel for Business - 148

- Using Excel for financial analysis - 149
- Creating and managing budgets - 152
- Forecasting sales and expenses - 156
- Using Excel for project management and tracking - 160

About the Author:

Santosh Cholle writes book, which, considering while you're reading this, makes a perfect sense.

Born in Mumbai, began writing in 2022 and has contributed to his debut book 'The Excel Edge'. 'The Derivatives Edge is his second book.

With the purchase of his first stock by selling his bicycle 31 years back and currently actively trading in derivatives, Santosh has poured his vast experience in this one book.

His work across multiple disciplines broadly addresses nuances of Personal Finance, MS Office & Technology.

He holds a Masters in Business Administration degree from IIM Pune and a Bachelor's degree in Arts from the University of Mumbai.

He currently lives with his wife and family in Pune and loves travelling across the globe.

Also by Santosh Cholle

The Derivatives Edge – Taming the Wild Beast of Finance

To my Parents, Son

&

To all Excel Masters & Learners

THE EXCEL EDGE

Mastering Spreadsheets for Business and Beyond

Santosh Cholle

Chapter 1:

Getting Started with Excel

• Introduction to Excel and its interface

Introduction to Excel and its interface is the first topic that one should learn when starting to use Excel. Excel is a spreadsheet software application that allows users to organize, calculate, and analyse data using various features and tools. It is a part of the Microsoft Office suite of applications, and it is widely used in business, education, and personal applications.

When you first open Excel, you will be presented with a blank workbook. The interface consists of various elements, which are:

1. **Title Bar**: It displays the name of the workbook and the application.

2. **Ribbon:** It is the main toolbar that contains all the commands and options to work with Excel. The ribbon is divided into tabs, and each tab contains groups of related commands.

3. **Quick Access Toolbar:** It is a customizable toolbar that contains frequently used commands. By default, it includes commands like Save, Undo, and Redo.

4. **Formula Bar:** It displays the contents of the active cell. You can use it to enter or edit data and formulas.

5. **Worksheet Area:** It is the main area where you can enter and view data. It consists of rows and columns, and each intersection of a row and column is called a cell.

6. **Status Bar:** It displays information about the current status of Excel, such as the page number, selected cells, and formula calculation mode.

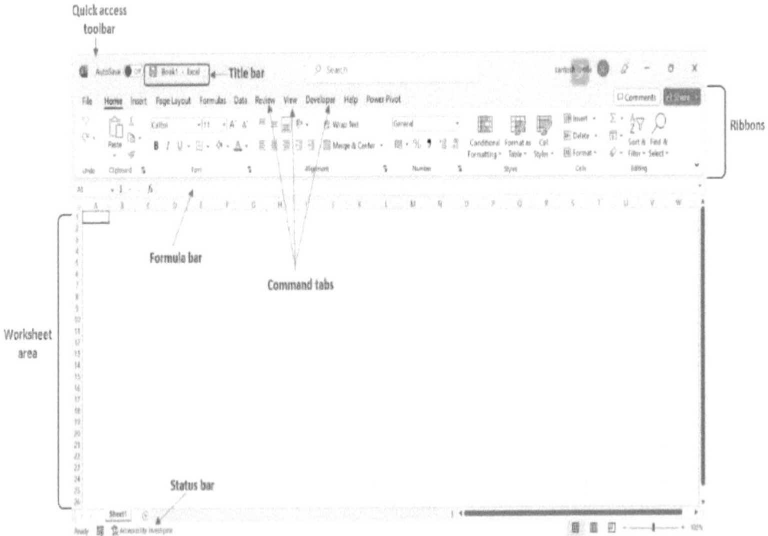

To start using Excel, you need to know how to enter data into cells. You can simply click on a cell and start typing. You can also use the arrow keys to move to the next cell. To enter a formula, you need to start with an equal sign (=) and then enter the formula using cell references and operators.

Excel has various formatting options that allow you to change the appearance of cells, such as font, colour, alignment, and borders. You can also format cells for numbers, dates, and times.

In conclusion, Excel is a powerful tool for organizing and analysing data. Understanding its interface and basic features is essential to using it effectively. By mastering the basics, you can then move on to more advanced features such as formulas, functions, charts, and pivot tables.

• Creating and saving a new workbook

Creating and saving a new workbook is one of the essential skills you need to learn when using Excel. A workbook is a file that contains one or more worksheets, and each worksheet contains rows and columns of data. Here's how you can create and save a new workbook:

1. **Open Excel:** To open Excel, click on the Excel icon on your desktop or search for it in the Start menu.

2. **Create a new workbook:** Once Excel is open, click on "File" on the top left corner and select "New.". You can also use the keyboard shortcut "Ctrl + N." A new workbook will open with one worksheet.

3. **Add worksheets:** If you need to add more worksheets to the workbook, click on the "+" icon on the bottom left corner of the screen or right-click on an existing worksheet and select "Insert." You can also use the keyboard shortcut "Shift + F11."

4. **Enter data:** Once you have created a new workbook, you can start entering data. Click on a cell and start typing, or you can copy and paste data from other sources.

5. **Save the workbook:** To save the workbook, click on "File" and select "Save As." Choose the location where you want to save the file, give it a name, and select the file type. Excel offers several file types, including .xlsx, .xls, and .csv.

6. **Manage versions:** Excel also allows you to manage versions of your workbook. You can save a copy of the workbook as a different version or use the "Save As" feature to create a new file with a different name.

7. **Auto-save and recover:** Excel has an auto-save feature that automatically saves your workbook every few minutes. If Excel crashes or your computer shuts down unexpectedly, you can recover your work by opening Excel and clicking on "File" and then "Recent."

In conclusion, creating and saving a new workbook in Excel is a simple process. By following these steps, you can create a new workbook, add worksheets, enter data, and save the workbook in various file formats. Excel also offers features to manage versions and recover work in case of unexpected disruptions.

• Formatting options

Formatting options in Excel allow you to customize the appearance of your data and make it more visually appealing and easier to read. Here are some of the formatting options available in Excel:

1. **Font:** You can change the font type, size, and colour of your text. You can also apply effects such as bold, italic, and underline.

2. **Alignment:** You can align text horizontally and vertically within a cell. You can also adjust the indentation and text direction.

3. **Number Formatting:** You can format numbers with different decimal places, currency symbols, and percentage signs. You can also add commas and negative number indicators.

4. **Conditional Formatting:** You can use conditional formatting to apply formatting to cells based on their values. For example, you can highlight cells that contain values above or below a certain threshold.

5. **Cell Borders:** You can add borders around cells to make them stand out. You can also customize the border style and colour.

6. **Fill Colour:** You can change the colour of cell backgrounds to make them stand out. You can also apply gradients or patterns.

7. **Styles:** You can apply pre-designed styles to cells, including combinations of font, alignment, and formatting options.

   Excel offers many other formatting options, including themes, table styles, and sparklines. You can access most of these options from the "Home" tab on the ribbon. Additionally, Excel offers many keyboard shortcuts that can speed up your formatting tasks.

   In conclusion, formatting options in Excel can significantly improve the visual appeal and readability of your data. Excel offers many formatting options, including font, alignment, number formatting, conditional formatting, cell borders, fill colour, and styles. By using these options, you can create professional-looking spreadsheets that are easy to understand and interpret.

• Entering and editing data

Entering and editing data in Excel is one of the fundamental skills you need to master in order to use the software effectively. Here are some tips for entering and editing data in Excel:

1. **Select a cell:** To enter data in a cell, first select the cell by clicking on it with your mouse or by using the arrow keys on your keyboard.

2. **Enter data:** Once the cell is selected, you can start typing in the data. You can also copy and paste data from other sources, such as a text document or another spreadsheet.

3. **Edit data:** To edit data in a cell, simply click on the cell and make your changes. You can also use the arrow keys to move to the part of the cell you want to edit.

4. **Delete data:** To delete data from a cell, select the cell and press the "Delete" key on your keyboard. You can also right-click on the cell and select "Delete" from the menu.

5. **Fill down:** If you have a long list of data to enter, you can use the "Fill Down" feature to quickly copy the data down the column. Simply enter the first value in the cell, select the cell, and then click and drag the bottom right corner of the cell down the column.

6. **AutoCorrect:** Excel has an AutoCorrect feature that can help you correct common typing mistakes automatically. For

example, if you type "teh" instead of "the," Excel can automatically correct it for you.

7. **Data validation:** You can use data validation to ensure that users enter valid data in a cell. For example, you can restrict users to entering only numbers or dates.

8. **Spell check:** Excel has a built-in spell check feature that can help you catch spelling errors in your data.

In conclusion, entering and editing data in Excel is a basic skill that you need to master in order to use the software effectively. By following these tips, you can enter data quickly and accurately, and make sure your data is error-free.

Chapter 2:

Working with Formulas and Functions

• Understanding basic arithmetic operators

Excel is a powerful spreadsheet program that includes a wide range of arithmetic operators to help you perform basic calculations on your data. Understanding these operators is important for working with Excel effectively. Here are the basic arithmetic operators in Excel and how to use them:

1. **Addition (+):** The addition operator is used to add two or more values together. For example, if you want to add the values in cells A1 and B1 together, you would enter the formula =A1+B1 in another cell.

2. **Subtraction (-):** The subtraction operator is used to subtract one value from another. For example, if you want to subtract the value in cell B1 from the value in cell A1, you would enter the formula =A1-B1 in another cell.

3. **Multiplication** (): The multiplication operator is used to multiply two or more values together. For example, if you want to multiply the values in cells A1 and B1 together, you would enter the formula =A1B1 in another cell.

4. **Division (/):** The division operator is used to divide one value by another. For example, if you want to divide the value in cell A1 by the value in cell B1, you would enter the formula =A1/B1 in another cell.

5. **Exponentiation (^):** The exponentiation operator is used to raise a number to a power. For example, if you want to calculate 2 to the power of 3, you would enter the formula =2^3 in another cell.

6. **Modulus (%):** The modulus operator returns the remainder of a division operation. For example, if you want to find the remainder when 10 is divided by 3, you would enter the formula =10%3 in another cell. The result would be 1, since 10 divided by 3 equals 3 with a remainder of 1.

7. **Concatenation (&):** The concatenation operator is used to combine two or more text strings into one. For example, if you have the text "Hello" in cell A1 and the text "World" in cell B1, you can combine them using the formula =A1&B1, which would result in the text "HelloWorld".

8. **Negation (-):** The negation operator is used to change the sign of a number. For example, if you have the number 5 in cell A1, you can make it negative by entering the formula =-A1 in another cell, which would result in the value -5.

9. **Percentages (%):** Excel includes several operators for working with percentages, including the percent sign (%) and the percent rank operator (PERCENTRANK). The percent sign is used to convert a number to a percentage, while the PERCENTRANK function is used to calculate the relative position of a value in a range of data as a percentage.

10. **Absolute values (ABS):** The ABS function is used to return the absolute value of a number. For example, if you have the number -5 in cell A1, you can find its absolute value by

entering the formula =ABS(A1) in another cell, which would result in the value 5.

11. **Rounding functions (ROUND, ROUNDUP, ROUNDDOWN):** Excel includes several functions for rounding numbers to a specified number of decimal places. The ROUND function rounds a number to the nearest specified number of decimal places, while the ROUNDUP function always rounds up and the ROUNDDOWN function always rounds down.

12. **Logarithms and exponentials (LOG, EXP):** Excel includes several functions for working with logarithms and exponentials. The LOG function returns the logarithm of a number to a specified base, while the EXP function returns e raised to the power of a specified number.

In conclusion, understanding advanced arithmetic operators in Excel is important for performing more complex calculations and working with a wider range of data types, such as text and percentages. By using these operators and functions, you can perform a variety of calculations, from concatenating text strings to finding the absolute value of a number or rounding it to a specified number of decimal places.

• Writing simple formulas

Excel allows you to write simple formulas that perform calculations on numerical data in your spreadsheet. These formulas are built using basic arithmetic operators, such as +, -, *, /, and ^, which represent addition, subtraction, multiplication, division, and exponentiation respectively. Here are some examples of simple formulas in Excel:

1. **Addition**: The simplest formula in Excel is an addition formula. To add two numbers, simply type the equals sign (=) followed by the two numbers separated by a plus sign (+). For example, to add the numbers 5 and 10, type the formula =5+10 into a cell and press Enter. The result should be 15.

2. **Subtraction:** To subtract two numbers, type the equals sign followed by the first number minus the second number. For example, to subtract 10 from 5, type the formula =5-10 and press Enter. The result should be -5.

3. **Multiplication:** To multiply two numbers, type the equals sign followed by the first number multiplied by the second number. For example, to multiply 5 by 10, type the formula =5*10 and press Enter. The result should be 50.

4. **Division:** To divide two numbers, type the equals sign followed by the first number divided by the second number. For example, to divide 10 by 5, type the formula =10/5 and press Enter. The result should be 2.

5. **Exponentiation:** To raise a number to a power, type the equals sign followed by the base number raised to the

exponent. For example, to raise 2 to the power of 3, type the formula =2^3 and press Enter. The result should be 8.

6. **Using cell references:** Instead of typing in numbers directly, you can also use cell references in your formulas. Simply type the equals sign followed by the cell reference, and then use the appropriate operator to perform the calculation. For example, to add the values in cells A1 and A2, type the formula =A1+A2 and press Enter.

   In conclusion, writing simple formulas in Excel is an essential skill that allows you to perform basic arithmetic operations on numerical data in your spreadsheet. By using basic arithmetic operators and cell references, you can create formulas that perform a variety of calculations, from adding and subtracting to multiplying, dividing, and raising numbers to a power.

• Introduction to functions

Functions are pre-built formulas in Excel that can perform specific tasks. Here are some of the most commonly used functions in Excel:

1. **SUM:** This function adds up a range of numbers. For example, if you want to add up the values in cells A1 to A5, you would use the formula =SUM(A1:A5).

2. **SUMIFS:** This function allows you to add up values based on multiple criteria. For example, if you want to add up the values in cells A1 to A5, but only if the corresponding cells in B1 to B5 contain the word "Apples", you would use the formula =SUMIFS(A1:A5, B1:B5, "Apples").

3. **SUMPRODUCT:** This function multiplies corresponding values in two or more arrays and then adds the products together. For example, if you have two arrays, A1:A5 and B1:B5, and you want to find the sum of the products of the corresponding values, you would use the formula =SUMPRODUCT(A1:A5, B1:B5).

4. **RIGHT:** This function returns a specified number of characters from the right side of a string. For example, if you want to extract the last three characters from the text in cell A1, you would use the formula =RIGHT(A1, 3).

5. **LEFT:** This function returns a specified number of characters from the left side of a string. For example, if you want to

extract the first four characters from the text in cell A1, you would use the formula =LEFT(A1, 4).

6. **MIN:** This function returns the smallest value in a range of cells. For example, if you want to find the smallest value in cells A1 to A5, you would use the formula =MIN(A1:A5).

7. **MAX:** This function returns the largest value in a range of cells. For example, if you want to find the largest value in cells A1 to A5, you would use the formula =MAX(A1:A5).

8. **MID:** This function returns a specified number of characters from the middle of a string. For example, if you want to extract three characters from the middle of the text in cell A1, starting at the fourth character, you would use the formula =MID(A1, 4, 3).

9. **AVERAGE:** This function returns the average value of a range of cells. For example, if you want to find the average value of cells A1 to A5, you would use the formula =AVERAGE(A1:A5).

10. **AVERAGEIFS:** This function allows you to find the average value of a range of cells based on multiple criteria. For example, if you want to find the average value of cells A1 to A5, but only if the corresponding cells in B1 to B5 contain the word "Apples", you would use the formula =AVERAGEIFS(A1:A5, B1:B5, "Apples").

11. **COUNT:** This function counts the number of cells in a range that contain numbers. For example, if you want to count the number of cells in cells A1 to A5 that contain numbers, you would use the formula =COUNT(A1:A5).

12. **COUNTIFS:** This function allows you to count the number of cells in a range based on multiple criteria. For example, if you want to count the number of cells in cells A1 to A5, but only if the corresponding cells in B1 to B5 contain the word "Apples", you would use the formula =COUNTIFS(A1:A5, B1:B5, "Apples").
13. **VLOOKUP Function:** The VLOOKUP function stands for Vertical Lookup. This function allows you to search for a value in the first column of a table and return a corresponding value in the same row from another column in the table. It has the following syntax:

    =VLOOKUP(lookup_value,table_array,col_index_num,[range_lookup])

    The arguments of the VLOOKUP function are:

- **lookup_value:** the value to be searched for in the first column of the table
- **table_array**: the table containing the data to be searched and the result to be returned
- **col_index_num**: the column number in the table from which to return the result
- **range_lookup:** an optional argument that specifies whether an exact match is required or not. If it is set to **TRUE** or omitted, an approximate match is allowed. If it is set to **FALSE**, an exact match is required.

Example:

Suppose you have a table containing a list of products and their prices, and you want to look up the price of a particular product. You can use the VLOOKUP function to do this as follows:

1. Enter the product name in a cell (e.g., "Product A") and the VLOOKUP function in another cell.

2. Specify the lookup value as the product name and the table array as the range containing the product names and prices.

3. Specify the column number of the price column as the col_index_num argument.

4. Set the range_lookup argument to **FALSE** to ensure an exact match is made.

   The formula would be:

   =VLOOKUP("Product A",A2:B10,2,FALSE)

   This would return the price of "Product A" in the table.

14. **HLOOKUP Function:** The HLOOKUP function stands for Horizontal Lookup. It is similar to the VLOOKUP function, but it searches for a value in the first row of a table and returns a corresponding value from another row in the same column. Its syntax is similar to the VLOOKUP function, but the arguments are arranged differently.

    Example:

    Suppose you have a table containing a list of products and their prices, and you want to look up the price of a particular product by specifying its category. You can use the HLOOKUP function to do this as follows:

1. Enter the category name in a cell (e.g., "Category A") and the HLOOKUP function in another cell.

2. Specify the lookup value as the category name and the table array as the range containing the category names and prices.

3. Specify the row number of the row containing the prices as the row_index_num argument.

4. Set the range_lookup argument to **FALSE** to ensure an exact match is made.

   The formula would be:

   =HLOOKUP("Category A",A1:B10,2,FALSE)

   This would return the price of the first product in the "Category A" row.

   The PMT and FV functions are both financial functions in Excel that are used for calculating loan payments and future values, respectively. Here's an overview of each function along with examples of how to use them:

15. **PMT Function:** The PMT function is used to calculate the periodic payment for a loan, given the interest rate, number of payments, and principal amount. The syntax for the PMT function is as follows:

    PMT(rate, nper, pv, [fv], [type])

- rate: The interest rate per period. It can be either a decimal or a reference to a cell containing the interest rate.
- nper: The total number of payments for the loan.
- pv: The present value, or the amount of the loan.
- [fv]: (optional) The future value, or the remaining balance of the loan after the final payment. If omitted, it is assumed to be 0.
- [type]: (optional) Specifies whether payments are due at the beginning (type=1) or end (type=0) of the period. If omitted, it is assumed to be 0.

  Example: Suppose you take out a $10,000 loan for 5 years at an interest rate of 5% per year. You want to know the monthly payment required to pay off the loan. You can use the PMT function to calculate this as follows:

  =PMT(5%/12, 5*12, 10000)

  This formula returns a value of -$188.71, indicating that you would need to make monthly payments of $188.71 for 5 years to pay off the loan.

16. **FV Function:** The FV function is used to calculate the future value of an investment or a savings account, given the present value, interest rate, and number of periods. The syntax for the FV function is as follows:

    FV(rate, nper, pmt, [pv], [type])

- rate: The interest rate per period. It can be either a decimal or a reference to a cell containing the interest rate.
- nper: The total number of periods for the investment.
- pmt: The periodic payment made during each period.
- [pv]: (optional) The present value, or the initial investment. If omitted, it is assumed to be 0.
- [type]: (optional) Specifies whether payments are due at the beginning (type=1) or end (type=0) of the period. If omitted, it is assumed to be 0.

Example: Suppose you invest $1,000 for 10 years at an annual interest rate of 6%. You want to know the future value of this investment after 10 years. You can use the FV function to calculate this as follows:

=FV(6%/12, 10*12, -1000)

This formula returns a value of $1,948.22, indicating that your investment would be worth $1,948.22 after 10 years.

• Using absolute and relative cell references

In Excel, cell references are used to identify the location of a cell in a worksheet. These cell references can be either absolute or relative. Understanding the difference between the two types of references is important as it can affect the behaviour of a formula when it is copied or moved to different cells.

Relative cell references are the default type of reference used in Excel. When a formula containing a relative cell reference is copied or moved to a different cell, the reference changes relative to its new location. For example, if you have a formula in cell A1 that refers to cell B1, and you copy the formula to cell A2, the formula in cell A2 will refer to cell B2 instead of B1.

Absolute cell references, on the other hand, always refer to the same cell regardless of where the formula is copied or moved. To make a cell reference absolute, you need to add a dollar sign ($) before the column letter and/or row number. For example, if you have a formula in cell A1 that refers to cell B1, and you want to make the reference to B1 absolute, you would change the formula to refer to B1.

Using a mixed cell reference allows you to keep one part of the reference relative while making the other part absolute. For example, if you have a formula in cell A1 that refers to cell B1 and you want to make the column reference absolute but keep the row reference relative, you would change the reference to $B1.

Here's an example of how absolute and relative cell references can be used in a formula:

Suppose you have a table of sales data with the following columns: Product, Price, Quantity, and Total. You want to calculate the total revenue for each product. You can use the following formula:

=Price * Quantity

If you copy this formula to the cells below, the references will change accordingly. For example, if you copy the formula to the cell below it, the formula will become:

=Price * Quantity

However, if you make the references to Price and Quantity absolute, the formula will always refer to those cells regardless of where it is copied. To do this, you would modify the formula to:

=B2 * C2

When you copy this formula to the cells below, the references will remain the same, and the correct calculation will be made for each row.

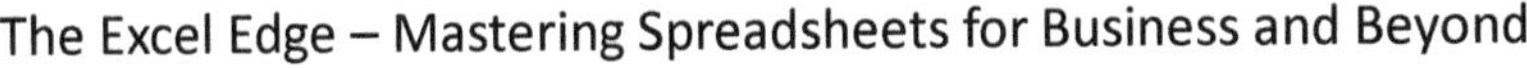

Chapter 3:

Managing Worksheets and Workbooks

• Renaming, moving, and deleting worksheets

Excel allows users to manage multiple worksheets within a workbook. In this section, we will cover the basic operations of renaming, moving, and deleting worksheets.

Renaming Worksheets: To rename a worksheet in Excel, you can right-click on the worksheet tab at the bottom of the screen and select "Rename" or simply double-click on the worksheet tab. You can then enter a new name for the worksheet and press Enter.

Moving Worksheets: To move a worksheet to a new location within the same workbook, you can drag and drop the worksheet tab to a new location. You can also right-click on the worksheet tab and select "Move or Copy" to open a dialog box where you can select the new location for the worksheet.

Deleting Worksheets: To delete a worksheet, you can right-click on the worksheet tab and select "Delete" or simply press the "Delete" key on your keyboard. Excel will prompt you to confirm the deletion of the worksheet before permanently deleting it.

It is important to note that deleting a worksheet will also delete any data and formatting that is contained within it. Therefore, it is always a good practice to create a backup of your workbook before deleting any worksheets.

In addition to the basic operations, Excel also provides several advanced features for managing and organizing worksheets. For example, you can group multiple worksheets together, create a summary worksheet that references data from other worksheets, and hide or unhide worksheets as needed.

To group multiple worksheets together, you can select the first worksheet, hold down the "Shift" key, and then select the last worksheet in the group. You can then perform operations on the entire group of worksheets, such as copying or formatting.

To create a summary worksheet that references data from other worksheets, you can use the "SUM" function or other appropriate functions to aggregate data from the various worksheets. You can also use a PivotTable to summarize and analyse data from multiple worksheets.

To hide or unhide worksheets, you can right-click on the worksheet tab and select "Hide" or "Unhide". Hidden worksheets will not be visible in the worksheet tabs at the bottom of the screen, but can still be accessed by other worksheets or through the "Unhide" command.

By mastering these basic and advanced operations for managing and organizing worksheets, you can greatly enhance your productivity and efficiency in Excel.

• Creating and managing workbooks

Excel provides various features to create and manage workbooks that contain multiple worksheets or charts. In this section, we will discuss the steps involved in creating and managing workbooks in Excel.

Creating a new workbook: To create a new workbook, follow the steps below:

1. Click on the "File" menu in the top left corner of the Excel window.
2. Select "New" from the list of options.
3. Choose "Blank workbook" or select a template from the available options.

Saving a workbook: After you have created a workbook, it is important to save it to avoid losing any data. Follow the steps below to save a workbook:

1. Click on the "File" menu.
2. Select "Save As".
3. Choose the location where you want to save the file.
4. Enter a name for the file in the "File name" field.
5. Select the file format in the "Save as type" field.

6. Click on "Save".

Opening an existing workbook: To open an existing workbook, follow the steps below:

1. Click on the "File" menu.
2. Select "Open".
3. Choose the location where the file is saved.
4. Select the file.
5. Click on "Open".

Managing worksheets: A workbook can contain multiple worksheets. To manage worksheets, follow the steps below:

1. Right-click on a worksheet tab.
2. Choose an option from the list, such as "Rename", "Insert", "Delete", or "Move or Copy".
3. Follow the prompts to complete the action.

Managing workbooks: To manage workbooks, follow the steps below:

1. Click on the "File" menu.
2. Choose an option from the list, such as "Rename", "Move or Copy", or "Close".

3. Follow the prompts to complete the action.

   Using templates: Excel provides several templates that you can use to create new workbooks quickly. To use a template, follow the steps below:

1. Click on the "File" menu.

2. Select "New".

3. Choose a template from the list.

4. Follow the prompts to create a new workbook based on the template.

   In conclusion, creating and managing workbooks is an essential part of using Excel. With the help of the steps outlined above, you can easily create, save, open, and manage workbooks in Excel.

• Protecting and unprotecting worksheets and workbooks

In Excel, you can protect your worksheets and workbooks from unwanted changes or accidental modifications by setting up various types of protection. Let's take a closer look at how to protect and unprotect worksheets and workbooks in Excel.

Protecting a Worksheet:

1. Select the worksheet you want to protect.
2. Go to the "Review" tab in the Excel ribbon.
3. Click on "Protect Sheet" in the "Changes" group.
4. In the "Protect Sheet" dialog box, select the options you want to restrict.
5. Enter a password if you want to ensure that only authorized users can make changes.
6. Click "OK" to protect the worksheet.

Unprotecting a Worksheet:

1. Select the worksheet you want to unprotect.
2. Go to the "Review" tab in the Excel ribbon.

3. Click on "Unprotect Sheet" in the "Changes" group.
4. Enter the password if the worksheet is password protected.
5. Click "OK" to unprotect the worksheet.

Protecting a Workbook:

1. Go to the "File" tab in the Excel ribbon.
2. Click on "Info" and then on "Protect Workbook."
3. In the "Protect Workbook" dialog box, select the options you want to restrict.
4. Enter a password if you want to ensure that only authorized users can make changes.
5. Click "OK" to protect the workbook.

Unprotecting a Workbook:

1. Go to the "File" tab in the Excel ribbon.
2. Click on "Info" and then on "Protect Workbook."
3. Enter the password if the workbook is password protected.
4. Click "OK" to unprotect the workbook.

It is important to note that password protection in Excel is not fool proof and can be easily broken by determined individuals. Therefore, it is always advisable to keep a backup of important data and to use other security measures in addition to password protection.

• Using the Page Layout and Print options

Excel provides several page layout and print options to help you print your worksheets in a neat and organized way. Here are some of the main features of the Page Layout and Print options in Excel:

1. **Page Setup:** You can access the Page Setup dialog box by clicking on the Page Layout tab and then clicking on the Page Setup group. From here, you can set the paper size, orientation, margins, and scaling options for your worksheet.

2. **Print Titles:** If you have a large worksheet that spans multiple pages, you may want to repeat the column and row headers on each page to make it easier to read. To do this, go to the Page Layout tab and click on the Print Titles group. Then, select the rows or columns that you want to repeat on each page.

3. **Print Area:** If you only want to print a specific section of your worksheet, you can define a print area. To do this, select the range of cells that you want to print, then go to the Page Layout tab and click on the Print Area group. From here, you can either set the print area or clear the print area.

4. **Page Breaks:** Excel automatically inserts page breaks based on the size of your paper and the content of your worksheet. However, you can also manually insert page breaks to control how your worksheet is divided into pages. To do this, go to

the Page Layout tab and click on the Page Setup group. Then, click on the Breaks dropdown menu and select either Insert Page Break or Remove Page Break.

5. **Headers and Footers:** You can add headers and footers to your worksheet to display page numbers, dates, file names, or other information. To do this, go to the Insert tab and click on the Header & Footer group. From here, you can select a predefined header or footer or create a custom one.

6. **Print Preview:** Before you actually print your worksheet, you can preview it to see how it will look on paper. To do this, go to the File tab and click on Print. From here, you can select the printer and the print settings, and then click on the Print Preview button to see a preview of your worksheet.

These are some of the main features of the Page Layout and Print options in Excel. By using these tools, you can customize your worksheets for printing and make sure that they look professional and organized.

Chapter 4:

Formatting and Presenting Data

• Formatting cells for dates, numbers, and text

Formatting cells is an important aspect of working with Excel. It allows you to change the appearance of data within cells to make it easier to read and understand. There are various types of formatting options available in Excel, including date formatting, number formatting, and text formatting.

Date Formatting: Dates are often used in Excel to represent specific time frames. Excel offers a variety of date formatting options, including short date, long date, and custom date formats. To format a cell as a date, follow these steps:

1. Select the cells you want to format as dates.
2. Right-click on the cells and select "Format Cells."
3. In the Format Cells dialog box, click on the "Number" tab.
4. Select "Date" from the list of categories.
5. Choose the desired date format from the list of options.
6. Click "OK" to apply the formatting to the selected cells.

Number Formatting: Excel offers a range of number formatting options that allow you to display numbers in different ways, such as with commas, decimals, and currency symbols. To format a cell as a number, follow these steps:

1. Select the cells you want to format as numbers.
2. Right-click on the cells and select "Format Cells."
3. In the Format Cells dialog box, click on the "Number" tab.
4. Select "Number" from the list of categories.
5. Choose the desired number format from the list of options.
6. Click "OK" to apply the formatting to the selected cells.

Text Formatting: Excel also offers several text formatting options, such as font type, size, colour, and style. To format a cell as text, follow these steps:

1. Select the cells you want to format as text.
2. Right-click on the cells and select "Format Cells."
3. In the Format Cells dialog box, click on the "Alignment" tab.
4. Choose the desired text formatting options, such as font type, size, and colour.
5. Click "OK" to apply the formatting to the selected cells.

Conditional Formatting: Conditional formatting allows you to apply formatting to cells based on specific conditions. For example, you can use conditional formatting to highlight cells that contain values greater than a certain number or cells that meet certain criteria. To apply conditional formatting to cells, follow these steps:

1. Select the cells you want to apply conditional formatting to.
2. Click on the "Conditional Formatting" button in the "Home" tab.
3. Choose the desired formatting option, such as "Highlight Cell Rules" or "Top/Bottom Rules."
4. Set the specific conditions and formatting options for the selected cells.
5. Click "OK" to apply the conditional formatting to the selected cells.

These are some of the formatting options available in Excel. By using these options effectively, you can make your data more readable and visually appealing.

• Using Conditional Formatting to highlight data

Conditional formatting in Excel allows you to apply formatting to cells based on specific criteria or conditions. This feature can help you visually analyse data and highlight important information. In this section, we will elaborate on how to use conditional formatting in Excel with examples.

To apply conditional formatting, first, select the range of cells you want to apply the formatting to. Then, click on the "Conditional Formatting" button in the "Home" tab of the ribbon. This will open a drop-down menu with various formatting options.

There are several types of conditional formatting in Excel:

Highlight Cell Rules: This option allows you to apply formatting to cells based on their values. For example, you can use this feature to highlight all cells that contain values greater than a certain number. To do this, select the "Highlight Cell Rules" option from the drop-down menu and then choose the condition you want to apply.

Example: **Highlight all cells that contain values greater than 50.**

- Select the range of cells you want to apply the formatting to.

- Click on "Conditional Formatting" and select "Highlight Cell Rules".
- Choose "Greater Than" from the list of conditions.
- In the "Value" field, enter 50.
- Select the formatting you want to apply, such as a fill colour or font colour.
- Click "OK" to apply the formatting.

2. Top/Bottom Rules: This option allows you to highlight the top or bottom values in a range of cells. For example, you can use this feature to highlight the top 10 sales figures in a list.

   Example: **Highlight the top 10 sales figures in a list.**

- Select the range of cells you want to apply the formatting to.
- Click on "Conditional Formatting" and select "Top/Bottom Rules".
- Choose "Top 10 Items" from the list of options.
- Select the formatting you want to apply, such as a fill colour or font colour.
- Click "OK" to apply the formatting.

3. Data Bars: This option allows you to add a bar to each cell to represent its value. The length of the bar corresponds to the value in the cell.

Example: **Use data bars to visually represent the values in a range of cells.**

- Select the range of cells you want to apply the formatting to.
- Click on "Conditional Formatting" and select "Data Bars".
- Choose the type of data bar you want to use.
- Select the formatting you want to apply, such as a fill colour or border colour.
- Click "OK" to apply the formatting.

4. Colour Scales: This option allows you to apply a colour scale to a range of cells based on their values. The cells with the highest values will be coloured with the darkest shade, and the cells with the lowest values will be coloured with the lightest shade.

   Example: **Use colour scales to highlight the highest and lowest values in a range of cells.**

- Select the range of cells you want to apply the formatting to.
- Click on "Conditional Formatting" and select "Colour Scales".
- Choose the colour scale you want to use.
- Select the formatting you want to apply, such as a fill colour or font colour.
- Click "OK" to apply the formatting.

These are just a few examples of how you can use conditional formatting in Excel. There are many other options available, including icon sets and formula-based formatting. Experiment with these different features to find the ones that work best for your data.

• Creating and formatting tables

Creating and formatting tables in Excel is a powerful feature that allows you to organize and analyse large amounts of data. Tables make it easier to sort, filter, and analyse data quickly and efficiently. In this section, we will discuss how to create and format tables in Excel with examples.

Creating a Table:

To create a table in Excel, you need to follow these steps:

Step 1: Select the range of cells that you want to convert into a table.

Step 2: Click on the "Insert" tab in the ribbon.

Step 3: Click on the "Table" button in the "Tables" group.

Step 4: In the "Create Table" dialog box, select the "My table has headers" option if your table has headers. If your table does not have headers, then leave this option unchecked.

Step 5: Click on the "OK" button.

Your table is now created, and you can start formatting it.

Formatting a Table:

Once you have created a table in Excel, you can format it to make it more visually appealing and easier to read. Here are some ways to format a table in Excel:

1. **Apply a Table Style:** Excel provides a variety of built-in table styles that you can apply to your table. To apply a table style, follow these steps:

   Step 1: Click anywhere in the table.

   Step 2: Click on the "Design" tab in the ribbon.

   Step 3: Select the table style that you want to apply from the "Table Styles" group.

2. **Add Filters:** You can add filters to your table to make it easier to sort and filter data. To add filters, follow these steps:

   Step 1: Click anywhere in the table.

   Step 2: Click on the "Filter" button in the "Sort & Filter" group.

   Step 3: Click on the drop-down arrow in the column header that you want to filter.

   Step 4: Select the filter criteria that you want to apply.

3. **Change Column Widths:** You can change the width of columns in your table to make them wider or narrower. To change column widths, follow these steps:

   Step 1: Click and drag the column boundary to the right or left to adjust the width of the column.

4. **Add Totals:** You can add totals to your table to calculate the sum, average, or other function for a column of data. To add totals, follow these steps:

   Step 1: Click anywhere in the table.

   Step 2: Click on the "Design" tab in the ribbon.

   Step 3: Select the "Total Row" check box in the "Table Style Options" group.

   Step 4: Click on the drop-down arrow in the total row cell that you want to add a function to.

   Step 5: Select the function that you want to apply.

5. **Merge Cells:** You can merge cells in your table to combine multiple cells into one larger cell. To merge cells, follow these steps:

   Step 1: Select the cells that you want to merge.

   Step 2: Click on the "Merge & Centre" button in the "Alignment" group.

   Step 3: Select the merge option that you want to apply.

Conclusion:

In conclusion, creating and formatting tables in Excel is an essential skill that can save you a lot of time and effort when working with large amounts of data. By applying table styles, adding filters, changing column widths, adding totals, and merging cells, you can create a table that is visually appealing and easy to read.

• Adding charts and graphs to visualize data

Adding charts and graphs to visualize data is an important aspect of working with Excel. It can help you to communicate data effectively and quickly, and make it easier to understand trends and patterns in your data. In this section, we will discuss the steps involved in creating and formatting charts and graphs in Excel.

Step 1: **Select Data**

The first step in creating a chart or graph in Excel is to select the data that you want to include in the chart. Make sure that the data is arranged in columns or rows, with each column or row representing a separate series of data. The first row or column should contain the labels for each data series.

Step 2: **Insert Chart**

Once you have selected the data, click on the 'Insert' tab on the ribbon at the top of the screen. Click on the 'Charts' option and select the type of chart or graph you want to create. There are many different types of charts to choose from, such as column charts, line charts, pie charts, and more.

Step 3: **Customize Chart**

After you have inserted the chart, you can customize it by selecting various elements and changing their formatting. You can add or remove chart elements such as titles, axes, and legends, and change the colours and styles of the data series.

Step 4: **Change Chart Type**

You can also change the type of chart or graph after it has been created. Simply click on the chart and then click on the 'Change Chart Type' button in the 'Design' tab of the ribbon. From there, you can select a new chart type and format it as needed.

Step 5: **Add Data Labels and Axis Titles**

Adding data labels and axis titles can help to make your chart or graph easier to understand. To add data labels, select the chart and click on the 'Chart Elements' button. From there, you can select the data labels option and choose the location where you want to place them. You can also add axis titles by clicking on the 'Axis Titles' option and entering the desired text.

Step 6: **Save and Print Chart**

Once you have created and customized your chart or graph, you can save it as a separate file or include it in a report or presentation. You can also print the chart by selecting the 'Print' option in the 'File' menu.

In summary, creating charts and graphs in Excel involves selecting data, inserting a chart or graph, customizing it, changing its type, adding data labels and axis titles, and saving or printing it. By following these steps, you can effectively visualize your data and communicate your findings to others.

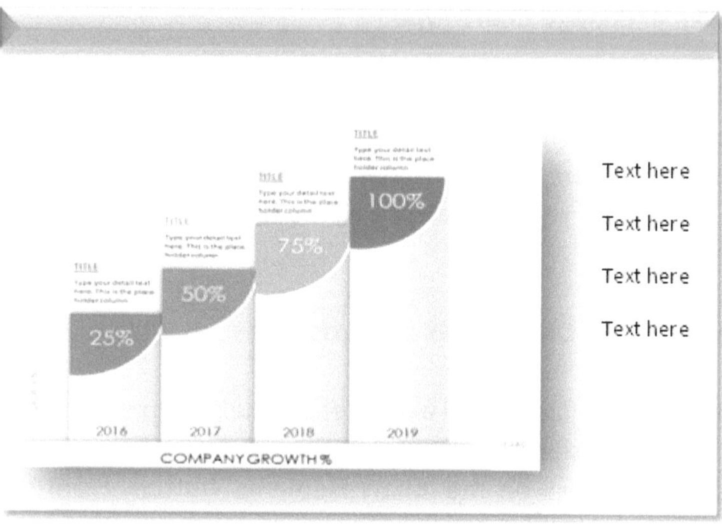

Chapter 5:

Advanced Formulas and Functions

• Advanced functions

Excel offers a wide range of advanced functions to help you with complex calculations and data analysis. Here are some of the most commonly used advanced functions in Excel along with examples:

1. **IF function:** The IF function allows you to test a condition and return one value if the condition is true and another value if the condition is false.

   Example: Suppose you want to calculate the bonus of employees based on their sales target. If an employee meets or exceeds the sales target, they get a bonus of 10% of their base salary, otherwise, they get no bonus. You can use the following IF function to calculate the bonus: =IF(B2>=C2,B2*10%,0)

2. **VLOOKUP function**: The VLOOKUP function allows you to look up a value in a table and return a corresponding value from the same row.

   Example: Suppose you have a table of employees' salaries and you want to find the salary of a specific employee. You can use the following VLOOKUP function: =VLOOKUP("John",A2:B6,2,FALSE)

3. **HLOOKUP function:** The HLOOKUP function is similar to VLOOKUP, but it looks up values in the first row of a table and returns the corresponding value from the same column.

   Example: Suppose you have a table of sales data for different regions and you want to find the sales data for a specific month. You can use the following HLOOKUP function: =HLOOKUP("Jan",A1:E4,3,FALSE)

4. **INDEX and MATCH functions:** The INDEX and MATCH functions are often used together to look up a value in a table and return a corresponding value from a different row and column.

   Example: Suppose you have a table of students' grades in different subjects and you want to find the grade of a specific student in a specific subject. You can use the following INDEX and MATCH functions: =INDEX(B2:F6,MATCH("John",A2:A6,0),MATCH("Math",B1:F1,0))

5. **SUMIF and SUMIFS functions:** The SUMIF and SUMIFS functions allow you to sum values that meet certain criteria.

   Example: Suppose you have a table of sales data for different products and you want to find the total sales for a specific product. You can use the following SUMIF function: =SUMIF(B2:B6,"Product A",C2:C6)

   If you want to sum values based on multiple criteria, you can use the SUMIFS function.

   Example: Suppose you have a table of sales data for different products and regions and you want to find the total sales for a specific product in a specific region. You can use the following SUMIFS function: =SUMIFS(C2:C6,B2:B6,"Product A",A2:A6,"Region 1")

6. **AVERAGEIF and AVERAGEIFS Functions:** The AVERAGEIF function is used to calculate the average of a range of cells that meet a certain criteria. The syntax of the AVERAGEIF function is as follows:

   =AVERAGEIF(range, criteria, [average_range])

   For example, the following formula calculates the average of all the values in range A1:A10 that are greater than 5:

   =AVERAGEIF(A1:A10, ">5")

   The AVERAGEIFS function is similar to AVERAGEIF, but allows you to specify multiple criteria. The syntax of the AVERAGEIFS function is as follows:

   =AVERAGEIFS(average_range, criteria_range1, criteria1, [criteria_range2], [criteria2], ...)

   For example, the following formula calculates the average of all the values in range A1:A10 that are greater than 5 and less than 10:

   =AVERAGEIFS(A1:A10, A1:A10, ">5", A1:A10, "<10")

• Using nested functions

Excel allows users to combine multiple functions in a single formula, also known as nested functions. By nesting one function within another, you can create more complex and sophisticated calculations that can handle a wider range of scenarios.

Here are some examples of nested functions in Excel:

1. **VLOOKUP with IF function:**

   =IF(VLOOKUP(A2,Table1,2,FALSE)="Yes","Pass","Fail")

   In this formula, the VLOOKUP function searches for a value in the first column of Table1 and returns the corresponding value in the second column. The IF function then checks whether the returned value is "Yes" and returns "Pass" if true and "Fail" if false.

2. **SUMIF with LEFT and IF functions:**

   =SUMIF(A2:A10,"=A*",IF(LEFT(B2:B10,1)="B",C2:C10,0))

   This formula uses the LEFT function to extract the first character from each value in column B, and the IF function checks whether the character is "B". If true, the SUMIF function adds up the corresponding values in column C.

3. **INDEX with MATCH and IFERROR functions:**

=IFERROR(INDEX(Table1,MATCH("Orange",Table1[Product],0),MATCH("Week 2",Table1[#Headers],0)),"Not Found")

This formula uses the MATCH function to find the row and column numbers for "Orange" and "Week 2" in Table1. The INDEX function then returns the value at the intersection of the specified row and column. The IFERROR function is used to display "Not Found" if the search term is not found.

4. **CONCATENATE with IF and TRIM functions:**

=IF(C2>0,CONCATENATE(A2," ",TRIM(B2)),"")

This formula checks whether the value in cell C2 is greater than 0. If true, the CONCATENATE function combines the values in cells A2 and B2 with a space between them, and the TRIM function removes any leading or trailing spaces. If false, the formula returns an empty string ("").

Nested functions in Excel can be very useful in performing complex calculations and data analysis tasks. However, it is important to keep the formula organized and easy to understand by breaking it down into smaller, simpler components.

• Working with arrays and array formulas

Working with arrays and array formulas in Excel can be a bit more complex than working with regular formulas, but can be extremely powerful in solving complex problems. An array formula performs a calculation on one or more sets of values, and returns either a single result or multiple results. The formula can be entered into one cell, but it will manipulate the values of an array of cells.

Arrays are typically represented as a range of cells. An array formula can take an array of values as an argument, and then perform an operation on those values. For example, you might use an array formula to calculate the average of a range of cells, or to find the maximum value in a range of cells.

Here are some examples of working with arrays and array formulas in Excel:

1. **Summing a range of cells using an array formula**:

   Suppose you have a range of cells from A1 to A10 that contains numeric values, and you want to sum them up. Instead of using the SUM function, you can use an array formula that sums up the range of cells.

   To do this, you would enter the formula "=SUM(A1:A10)" in a cell, but instead of pressing "Enter" to finish, you would press "Ctrl+Shift+Enter" to enter the formula as an array formula. This will enclose the formula in curly braces {}.

2. **Finding the maximum value in a range of cells using an array formula:**

   Suppose you have a range of cells from B1 to B10 that contains numeric values, and you want to find the maximum value. Again, instead of using the MAX function, you can use an array formula to find the maximum value.

   To do this, you would enter the formula "=MAX(B1:B10)" in a cell, but instead of pressing "Enter" to finish, you would press "Ctrl+Shift+Enter" to enter the formula as an array formula.

3. **Using the IF function in an array formula:**

   Suppose you have a range of cells from C1 to C10 that contains numeric values, and you want to find all the values that are greater than 5. You can use the IF function in combination with an array formula to accomplish this.

   To do this, you would enter the formula "=IF(C1:C10>5, C1:C10, "")" in a cell, but instead of pressing "Enter" to finish, you would press "Ctrl+Shift+Enter" to enter the formula as an array formula. This will return an array of values, where any value that is not greater than 5 will be blank.

4. **Using the INDEX and MATCH functions in an array formula:**

   Suppose you have a range of cells from D1 to D10 that contains a list of names, and you want to find the position of a specific name in the list. You can use the INDEX and MATCH functions in combination with an array formula to accomplish this.

To do this, you would enter the formula "=MATCH("John",D1:D10,0)" in a cell to find the position of the name "John" in the list. Instead of pressing "Enter" to finish, you would press "Ctrl+Shift+Enter" to enter the formula as an array formula. Then, you could use the INDEX function to find the corresponding value in another column, like so: "=INDEX(E1:E10,MATCH("John",D1:D10,0))".

These are just a few examples of the many ways you can use arrays and array formulas in Excel to manipulate and analyse your data. With practice, you can become proficient in using these advanced features to perform complex calculations and solve challenging problems.

• Using logical functions like AND, OR, and NOT

Logical functions are an important aspect of Excel, as they allow you to analyse and manipulate data based on certain conditions. The three main logical functions in Excel are AND, OR, and NOT.

The AND function returns TRUE if all the arguments are TRUE, and FALSE otherwise. For example, suppose you have a table of students and their grades for three different tests. You can use the AND function to determine which students scored above 80% on all three tests. The formula would be:

=AND(B2>80%, C2>80%, D2>80%)

Here, B2, C2, and D2 are the cells containing the grades for each test, and 80% is the threshold for passing. If all three grades are above 80%, the formula returns TRUE.

The OR function returns TRUE if at least one of the arguments is TRUE, and FALSE otherwise. Continuing with the same example, you can use the OR function to determine which students scored above 80% on at least one of the tests. The formula would be:

=OR(B2>80%, C2>80%, D2>80%)

If any of the three grades are above 80%, the formula returns TRUE.

The NOT function returns the opposite of the argument, that is, it returns TRUE if the argument is FALSE, and FALSE if the argument is TRUE. For example, suppose you have a table of employees and their salaries, and you want to identify employees whose salary is less than 50,000. You can use the NOT function to invert the logical test:

```
=NOT(B2>=50000)
```

Here, B2 is the cell containing the employee's salary. If the salary is less than 50,000, the formula returns TRUE.

In addition to these basic logical functions, Excel also has several other logical functions that can be used for more complex analyses. For example, the IF function allows you to specify different actions depending on whether a condition is met or not. The IFERROR function allows you to specify a value to return if an error occurs. The CONCATENATE function allows you to join two or more strings of text together.

Overall, logical functions are a powerful tool in Excel for analysing and manipulating data based on certain conditions. By using these functions, you can quickly and easily identify patterns and trends in your data, and make informed decisions based on those insights.

Chapter 6:

Working with Pivot Tables

• Understanding PivotTables and their benefits

PivotTables are one of the most powerful tools in Excel, allowing users to analyse and summarize large amounts of data quickly and easily. A PivotTable is a dynamic table that allows you to summarize, analyse and manipulate large amounts of data quickly and easily. You can create a PivotTable from a range of data, and then filter, sort, and analyse the data in various ways.

Benefits of using PivotTables:

- PivotTables allow you to summarize large amounts of data quickly and easily.
- You can easily change the layout of your data in a PivotTable, without having to re-enter the data or modify your original data source.
- PivotTables allow you to filter, sort, and group your data in various ways, giving you greater control over your data analysis.
- You can easily create charts and graphs from your PivotTable data, making it easy to communicate your findings to others.

Creating a PivotTable:

1. Start by selecting the data range you want to use for your PivotTable.

2. From the Insert tab, select the PivotTable option.

3. In the Create PivotTable dialog box, select the location where you want to place your PivotTable.

4. Choose the fields you want to include in your PivotTable. These can include rows, columns, values, and filters.

5. Click OK to create your PivotTable.

Customizing a PivotTable:

Once you have created your PivotTable, you can customize it in various ways:

1. Change the layout: You can easily change the layout of your PivotTable by dragging and dropping fields to different areas of the PivotTable.

2. Group data: You can group data in your PivotTable by date, text, or numerical ranges.

3. Filter data: You can filter data in your PivotTable by selecting specific criteria from the filter drop-down menus.

4. Format your PivotTable: You can format your PivotTable to make it more visually appealing by changing the font, colour, and borders.

5. Create charts and graphs: You can easily create charts and graphs from your PivotTable data by selecting the chart type you want to use from the Insert tab.

Example:

Suppose you have a large data set containing sales data for a company. You want to analyse the data to see which products are selling the most, and which regions are generating the most revenue.

To do this, you can create a PivotTable by following these steps:

1. Select the data range containing your sales data.

2. From the Insert tab, select the PivotTable option.

3. In the Create PivotTable dialog box, select the location where you want to place your PivotTable.

4. Choose the fields you want to include in your PivotTable. For example, you might include product name, region, and sales amount.

5. Click OK to create your PivotTable.

Once you have created your PivotTable, you can start analysing your data. You can group your data by product name to see which products are selling the most. You can also filter your data by region to see which regions are generating the most revenue.

You can also format your PivotTable to make it more visually appealing, by changing the font, colour, and borders. You can even create charts and graphs from your PivotTable data, to help you visualize your findings.

• Creating PivotTables from data

Creating PivotTables is a powerful feature in Excel that allows you to analyse and summarize large amounts of data quickly and easily. PivotTables can be created from a range of data and can be customized to show exactly the information you need.

To create a PivotTable in Excel, follow these steps:

1. Ensure that your data is in a table or range with column headings. You can use any Excel table or range, as long as it has headings for each column.

2. Select any cell within the data range.

3. Go to the "Insert" tab in the ribbon and click on the "PivotTable" button in the "Tables" group.

4. In the "Create PivotTable" dialog box, select the range of data that you want to use for the PivotTable.

5. Choose where you want to place the PivotTable. You can either create a new worksheet or place it on an existing worksheet.

6. Click "OK" to create the PivotTable.

Once you have created a PivotTable, you can start customizing it to show the data you want. Here are some examples of how to use the different features in PivotTables:

1. Row and column fields: These are the fields that determine the layout of the PivotTable. Drag a field to the "Row Labels" or "Column Labels" area to group your data by that field.

2. Value fields: These are the fields that are used to calculate values in the PivotTable. Drag a field to the "Values" area to calculate values for that field.

3. Filters: Filters allow you to focus on specific data in your PivotTable. Drag a field to the "Filters" area to filter by that field.

4. Grouping: Grouping allows you to group data by date or number ranges. Right-click on a date or number field and select "Group" to group the data.

5. Calculated fields: Calculated fields allow you to create new fields based on existing ones. Go to the "Fields, Items, & Sets" menu and select "Calculated Field" to create a new field.

6. Slicers: Slicers allow you to filter data in your PivotTable by selecting specific criteria. Go to the "Insert" tab and select "Slicer" to add a slicer to your PivotTable.

Overall, PivotTables are a powerful tool for analysing and summarizing data in Excel. By following the steps outlined above, you can create PivotTables and customize them to show exactly the information you need.

• Sorting, filtering, and grouping data in PivotTables

PivotTables in Excel are a powerful tool that allows users to analyse large amounts of data quickly and easily. One of the key benefits of PivotTables is the ability to sort, filter, and group data to create customized views of your data. In this section, we will explore these features in more detail with examples.

Sorting Data in PivotTables:

Sorting data in a PivotTable is an essential feature that enables users to sort data in ascending or descending order. Excel allows users to sort data based on values, labels, or custom lists.

For example, consider the following PivotTable that shows the sales data for different regions and products.

To sort the data based on the values, follow these steps:

1. Select the column that you want to sort.

2. Click on the "Sort Ascending" or "Sort Descending" button in the "Sort & Filter" group on the "Data" tab.

In the example above, if we sort the "Sum of Sales" column in descending order, we can quickly see which regions have the highest sales.

Filtering Data in PivotTables:

Filtering data in a PivotTable allows users to see a specific subset of data by hiding the rows or columns that do not meet the specified criteria. Excel provides several filtering options, including label filters, value filters, and advanced filters.

For example, consider the following PivotTable that shows the sales data for different regions and products.

To filter the data based on the values, follow these steps:

1. Click on the drop-down arrow next to the column header that you want to filter.

2. Select the values that you want to show or hide.

In the example above, if we want to see only the sales data for the "Bikes" product, we can select "Bikes" in the "Product" column's filter drop-down.

Grouping Data in PivotTables:

Grouping data in a PivotTable allows users to create customized views of their data by grouping data into meaningful categories. Excel provides several grouping options, including date and time grouping, text grouping, and number grouping.

For example, consider the following PivotTable that shows the sales data for different regions and dates.

To group the data by month, follow these steps:

1. Select the column that contains the dates you want to group.
2. Right-click on the selected cells and choose "Group" from the menu.
3. In the "Grouping" dialog box, select "Months" and click "OK."

In the example above, if we group the "Date" column by month, we can quickly see the total sales for each month.

Conclusion:

Sorting, filtering, and grouping data in PivotTables are powerful features that allow users to create customized views of their data quickly and easily. By using these features, users can gain valuable insights into their data and make informed decisions based on their analysis.

• Using PivotCharts to visualize PivotTable data

PivotCharts are graphical representations of PivotTables. They allow you to visualize the data in a PivotTable in different chart formats like bar, column, line, pie, etc. PivotCharts provide an easy way to see patterns and trends in your data that might be hard to identify in a PivotTable.

Creating a PivotChart

To create a PivotChart, follow these steps:

1. Click anywhere in the PivotTable that you want to create a chart from.

2. From the "PivotTable Analyse" or "PivotTable Design" tab, select "PivotChart".

3. Select the chart type you want to create from the list of available options.

4. Choose where to place the chart, either in a new sheet or as an object in the current sheet.

5. Click OK to create the chart.

Formatting a PivotChart

Once you've created a PivotChart, you can customize it to suit your needs. Here are some of the formatting options available in Excel:

1. **Chart Layout:** Choose from a variety of pre-designed layouts to arrange your chart elements, such as titles, axes, legends, and data labels.

2. **Chart Style:** Change the colour scheme and style of your chart to match your preferences or company branding.

3. **Chart Title:** Add a descriptive title to your chart to make it clear what the data represents.

4. **Axis Labels:** Customize the labels on the x and y axes to provide more information about the data being displayed.

5. **Legend:** Adjust the position and style of the legend to make it easier to read.

Using Filters and Slicers

Just like in PivotTables, you can use filters and slicers in PivotCharts to analyse specific data subsets. Filters allow you to show or hide specific data based on criteria you choose. Slicers provide a more user-friendly interface for filtering data. Slicers are interactive buttons that allow users to quickly filter data by clicking on the buttons.

To add a slicer to your PivotChart, follow these steps:

1. Select the PivotChart you want to add a slicer to.

2. From the "PivotTable Analyse" or "PivotTable Design" tab, select "Insert Slicer".
3. Choose the field that you want to use as a slicer.
4. Click OK to create the slicer.

Using PivotChart Tools

Excel provides a set of tools that are specific to PivotCharts. These tools allow you to further customize your chart and analyse your data. Some of the tools include:

1. **Analyse Tab:** Provides a set of tools for filtering, sorting, and manipulating your data.
2. **Design Tab:** Provides a set of tools for formatting your chart and changing its appearance.
3. **Move Chart:** Allows you to move the chart to a new sheet or location within the current sheet.
4. **Chart Elements:** Provides a list of chart elements that you can add or remove, such as titles, data labels, and axes.

Conclusion

PivotCharts are a powerful tool for visualizing data in Excel. They allow you to easily see patterns and trends in your data, making it easier to make decisions based on the data. By following the steps outlined in this section, you should be able to create and customize PivotCharts to meet your needs.

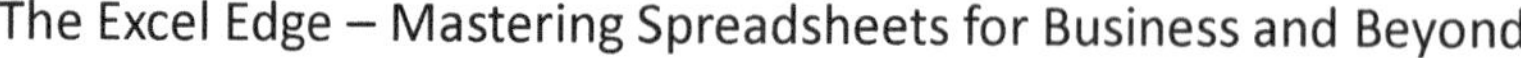

Chapter 7:

Using Macros for Automation

• Understanding macros and their benefits

Macros are automated actions in Excel that can save time and increase efficiency. They are a series of recorded actions that can be played back as many times as needed. Macros can be used to perform repetitive tasks, automate complex processes, and speed up data entry.

Benefits of using macros in Excel:

1. Saves time: Macros automate repetitive tasks, which saves a lot of time and effort.

2. Increases efficiency: Macros perform tasks accurately and quickly, which increases efficiency and reduces errors.

3. Easy to use: Macros can be created and used by anyone with basic knowledge of Excel.

4. Customizable: Macros can be customized to perform specific tasks according to user needs.

5. Consistent: Macros perform tasks consistently every time they are executed, which ensures accuracy and reduces errors.

Creating a macro in Excel:

1. To create a macro, first, click on the 'Developer' tab in the ribbon menu. If the 'Developer' tab is not visible, enable it by

clicking on 'File' > 'Options' > 'Customize Ribbon' and selecting the 'Developer' checkbox.

2. Click on the 'Record Macro' button in the 'Code' section of the 'Developer' tab.

3. In the 'Record Macro' dialog box, enter a name for the macro, select a shortcut key (optional), and choose where to save the macro (in a personal macro workbook, this workbook, or a new workbook).

4. Click on 'OK' to start recording the macro.

5. Perform the actions that you want to record in the macro. For example, if you want to automate the process of formatting a table, record the steps you take to format the table.

6. Once you have finished recording the macro, click on the 'Stop Recording' button in the 'Code' section of the 'Developer' tab.

Using a macro in Excel:

1. To use a macro, first, make sure that the 'Developer' tab is visible in the ribbon menu.

2. Click on the 'Macros' button in the 'Code' section of the 'Developer' tab.

3. Select the macro that you want to run from the list of macros.

4. Click on the 'Run' button to execute the macro.

Example:

Suppose you have a large amount of data in an Excel workbook, and you want to format it in a specific way. Instead of manually formatting the data every time, you can create a macro to automate the process.

To create the macro, follow the steps mentioned above. Once you have finished recording the macro, you can use it to format the data with just a few clicks.

To use the macro, open the workbook that contains the data you want to format. Click on the 'Macros' button in the 'Code' section of the 'Developer' tab, select the macro from the list of macros, and click on the 'Run' button. The macro will perform the formatting actions, and the data will be formatted in the way you specified.

Macros can be used for a variety of tasks, from automating simple formatting tasks to complex data analysis and modelling. They can be customized to fit specific needs and can save a significant amount of time and effort.

• Creating and running simple macros

Creating and running macros in Excel can save you a lot of time and effort, especially if you find yourself performing repetitive tasks. A macro is a series of instructions that can be executed with a single command or keystroke. In this section, we will explain how to create and run simple macros in Excel.

Creating a Macro in Excel:

1. Open a new or existing workbook in Excel.

2. Navigate to the Developer tab in the ribbon. If you do not see the Developer tab, you may need to enable it in Excel Options.

3. Click on the Record Macro button in the Code group.

4. In the Record Macro dialog box, enter a name for the macro in the Macro name field.

5. If you want to assign a keyboard shortcut to the macro, enter the shortcut in the Shortcut key field. You can also assign the macro to a button or shape on the worksheet.

6. Choose where to store the macro by selecting the location in the Store macro in dropdown list. You can store macros in the current workbook or in your Personal Macro Workbook.

7. Enter a description for the macro in the Description field (optional).

8. Click on OK to start recording the macro.

9. Perform the actions that you want the macro to automate. For example, you might format a range of cells, sort data, or apply filters.

10. When you are finished, click on the Stop Recording button in the Code group of the Developer tab.

Running a Macro in Excel:

- To run a macro, press the keyboard shortcut that you assigned to it, or click on the button or shape that you assigned the macro to.

- The macro will execute, performing the actions that you recorded.

Example of a Simple Macro in Excel:

Let's say that you have a large dataset in Excel and you need to format it in a specific way every time you receive new data. You can create a macro to automate the formatting process. Here is an example of a simple macro that formats a range of cells:

1. Open the worksheet that contains the data that you want to format.

2. Click on the Developer tab in the ribbon.

3. Click on the Record Macro button in the Code group.

4. In the Record Macro dialog box, enter a name for the macro (e.g. "Format Data").

5. Assign a keyboard shortcut to the macro (e.g. Ctrl + Shift + F).

6. Choose where to store the macro (e.g. This Workbook).

7. Click on OK to start recording the macro.

8. Select the range of cells that you want to format.

9. Click on the Format Painter button in the Clipboard group of the Home tab.

10. Click on the first cell where you want to apply the formatting.

11. The selected range of cells will be formatted. Click on the Stop Recording button in the Code group of the Developer tab.

    To run the macro, press the keyboard shortcut that you assigned to it (Ctrl + Shift + F in this example), or click on the button or shape that you assigned the macro to. The selected range of cells will be formatted automatically.

    Note that this is a simple example of a macro, and that you can create much more complex macros that perform a wide range of actions in Excel.

• Assigning macros to buttons and keyboard shortcuts

Assigning macros to buttons and keyboard shortcuts in Excel is a useful way to streamline and automate repetitive tasks. In this section, we will discuss how to assign macros to buttons and keyboard shortcuts in Excel.

Assigning Macros to Buttons: To assign a macro to a button, follow these steps:

1. Click on the Developer tab on the Ribbon.
2. Click on the Insert button in the Controls group.
3. Select the Button control from the menu.
4. Draw the button on the worksheet where you want it to appear.
5. In the Assign Macro dialog box, select the macro you want to assign to the button and click OK.
6. Edit the button text or appearance as desired.

Now, when you click the button, it will run the assigned macro.

Assigning Macros to Keyboard Shortcuts: To assign a macro to a keyboard shortcut, follow these steps:

1. Press ALT + F8 to open the Macros dialog box.

2. Select the macro you want to assign to a keyboard shortcut and click Options.

3. In the Macro Options dialog box, type a letter in the Shortcut Key box. This letter will be used as the keyboard shortcut to run the macro.

4. Click OK to close the Macro Options dialog box and then click Cancel to close the Macros dialog box.

   Now, when you press the keyboard shortcut you assigned, it will run the assigned macro.

   Examples: Let's say you have a macro that clears the contents of a range of cells, and you want to assign it to a button and a keyboard shortcut.

Assigning Macro to a Button:

1. Click on the Developer tab on the Ribbon.

2. Click on the Insert button in the Controls group.

3. Select the Button control from the menu.

4. Draw the button on the worksheet where you want it to appear.

5. In the Assign Macro dialog box, select the macro you want to assign to the button and click OK.

6. Edit the button text or appearance as desired.

   Now, when you click the button, it will run the macro that clears the contents of the range of cells.

   Assigning Macro to a Keyboard Shortcut:

1. Press ALT + F8 to open the Macros dialog box.
2. Select the macro that clears the contents of the range of cells and click Options.
3. In the Macro Options dialog box, type "C" in the Shortcut Key box. This will assign the Ctrl + C keyboard shortcut to the macro.
4. Click OK to close the Macro Options dialog box and then click Cancel to close the Macros dialog box.

   Now, when you press Ctrl + C, it will run the macro that clears the contents of the range of cells.

• Editing and deleting macros

In Excel, macros are a powerful tool that allows users to automate repetitive tasks and save time. Macros are a series of recorded actions that can be executed with the click of a button or keyboard shortcut. In this section, we will discuss how to edit and delete macros in Excel.

Editing Macros: To edit a macro in Excel, follow the steps below:

1. Press Alt+F11 to open the Visual Basic Editor.
2. In the Project Explorer window, select the module that contains the macro you want to edit.
3. Double-click the macro you want to edit. This will open the code window.
4. Make the desired changes to the macro code.
5. Press Alt+Q to return to the Excel workbook.

Deleting Macros: To delete a macro in Excel, follow the steps below:

1. Press Alt+F11 to open the Visual Basic Editor.
2. In the Project Explorer window, select the module that contains the macro you want to delete.

3. Select the macro you want to delete.

4. Press the Delete key on your keyboard.

5. Click "Yes" in the confirmation window that appears.

   It is important to note that once a macro is deleted, it cannot be recovered. Therefore, it is recommended that you make a backup of your Excel file before deleting any macros.

   Additionally, macros can also be deleted through the Excel interface by following these steps:

1. Click on the "View" tab in the Excel ribbon.

2. Click on the "Macros" dropdown menu.

3. Select "View Macros" from the dropdown menu.

4. In the "Macros" dialog box, select the macro you want to delete.

5. Click on the "Delete" button.

   In conclusion, editing and deleting macros in Excel can help you keep your workbook organized and efficient. It is important to use caution when editing or deleting macros, and to always make a backup of your Excel file before making any changes.

Chapter 8:

Collaborating and Sharing Workbooks

• Sharing workbooks with others

Sharing workbooks with others in Excel is a common task that is necessary in many workplaces. In this section, we will elaborate on the different ways you can share workbooks in Excel, along with their respective benefits and drawbacks.

1. **Emailing workbooks:** This is a simple way to share workbooks with others. You can email the workbook as an attachment, and the recipient can open it in their own version of Excel. However, this method has some drawbacks, such as the potential for version control issues if the recipient is using a different version of Excel than the sender, and the fact that email attachments can be blocked by spam filters.

2. **Saving workbooks to shared folders:** Another way to share workbooks is to save them to a shared folder, such as a network drive or cloud-based storage solution. This allows multiple people to access the workbook at the same time and collaborate on it in real-time. However, this method requires that all users have access to the shared folder, which may not always be possible.

3. **Sharing workbooks with OneDrive:** OneDrive is Microsoft's cloud-based storage solution, which allows users to save and share files with others. You can save an Excel workbook to OneDrive and share it with others, giving them permission to view or edit the file. This method offers the benefits of real-time collaboration, version control, and easy access, but it requires that all users have a OneDrive account.

4. **Sharing workbooks with SharePoint:** SharePoint is Microsoft's collaboration platform, which allows users to

share files, collaborate on documents, and manage projects. You can save an Excel workbook to a SharePoint site and share it with others, giving them permission to view or edit the file. This method offers the benefits of real-time collaboration, version control, and easy access, along with advanced collaboration features such as task tracking and document workflows.

In addition to these methods, there are also several other ways to share workbooks in Excel, such as using collaboration tools like Microsoft Teams, using third-party collaboration tools like Slack or Trello, or using Excel's built-in co-authoring features.

To share a workbook with others, follow these general steps:

1. Save the workbook to a location that is accessible to all users.

2. Determine the level of access that you want to grant to each user. You can choose to allow users to view the workbook, edit the workbook, or co-author the workbook in real-time.

3. Share the workbook with the appropriate users, using one of the methods outlined above.

4. Monitor the workbook to ensure that changes are being made correctly and that the workbook is not being overwritten by multiple users at the same time.

By following these steps, you can successfully share workbooks with others in Excel and collaborate effectively on important projects.

• Protecting and sharing specific cells or ranges

In Excel, you can protect and share specific cells or ranges to ensure that only authorized users can access and modify them. This can be useful when working with sensitive data or when collaborating on a workbook with multiple users.

Here are the steps to protect and share specific cells or ranges in Excel:

1. Select the cells or ranges that you want to protect.
2. Right-click on the selection and choose "Format Cells" from the drop-down menu.
3. In the "Format Cells" dialog box, go to the "Protection" tab.
4. Check the "Locked" box to lock the selected cells or ranges.
5. Click "OK" to close the dialog box.
6. Go to the "Review" tab in the Excel ribbon.
7. Click on "Protect Sheet" to open the "Protect Sheet" dialog box.
8. Check the boxes for the options you want to allow users to perform, such as "Select locked cells" or "Format cells".
9. Enter a password if you want to restrict access to the protected cells or ranges.

10. Click "OK" to close the dialog box and protect the sheet.

    Now, only authorized users can access and modify the protected cells or ranges, while other cells in the sheet remain editable. To unprotect the sheet, go to the "Review" tab, click on "Unprotect Sheet", and enter the password if necessary.

    Note that protecting and sharing specific cells or ranges in Excel does not prevent users from copying the data to another location or creating a new workbook with the same data. To prevent this, you may need to use additional security measures, such as encrypting the workbook or using digital signatures.

Encrypting workbooks and using digital signatures in Excel are important security features that can help protect your data from unauthorized access or tampering.

Encrypting a workbook means that you use a password to protect it from being opened or edited without authorization. You can encrypt a workbook by following these steps:

1. Click on "File" in the menu bar and select "Info".

2. Click on "Protect Workbook" and select "Encrypt with Password".

3. Enter a password in the "Password" field and click "OK".

4. Re-enter the password to confirm it and click "OK".

Once the workbook is encrypted, anyone who wants to open it will need to enter the password. Keep in mind that if you forget the password, there is no way to recover it, so make sure to keep a record of it somewhere safe.
Digital signatures are another way to ensure that your Excel workbook is secure. A digital signature is a mathematical scheme that verifies the authenticity and integrity of digital documents or messages. By adding a digital signature to your Excel workbook, you are essentially signing it to confirm that you are the author and that the data has not been tampered with.
To add a digital signature to your Excel workbook, follow these steps:

1. Click on "File" in the menu bar and select "Info".

2. Click on "Protect Workbook" and select "Add a Digital Signature".

3. Follow the prompts to create a digital signature.

Once you have added a digital signature to your workbook, anyone who opens it will see a notification that the workbook has been signed and can verify the authenticity of the signature.

Keep in mind that encryption and digital signatures are only effective if you keep your password safe and secure, and use strong authentication methods to protect your digital signature. It is also important to keep your software up to date with the latest security patches to minimize vulnerabilities.

• Using comments and track changes to collaborate

Excel provides several features that enable collaboration among users. Two such features are comments and track changes.

Comments: Comments allow users to add notes or feedback to a cell in the worksheet. This feature is especially useful when multiple users are working on the same worksheet, and one user needs to leave a note for others to view. To insert a comment, right-click on the cell where you want to insert a comment and select "Insert Comment." A text box will appear where you can enter your comment. Once you've entered your comment, you can close the text box. The cell will display a red triangle in the upper-right corner, indicating that a comment is attached. Hovering over the cell will display the comment.

Track Changes: Track changes is another feature that allows multiple users to collaborate on a worksheet. With track changes turned on, Excel will keep a record of all changes made to the worksheet. To turn on track changes, go to the "Review" tab in the Excel ribbon and click "Track Changes." You can then select the types of changes you want to track, such as insertions, deletions, and formatting changes. Once track changes is turned on, any changes made to the worksheet will be highlighted, and a comment box will appear indicating the user who made the change. You can then accept or reject changes made by other users.

Here's an example of how these features can be used in a collaborative setting:

Suppose a team of three users is working on a budget worksheet. User A is responsible for entering income data, user B is responsible for entering expenses, and user C is responsible for creating charts and graphs to visualize the data.

User A enters the income data in the worksheet and adds comments to explain any unusual entries. User B then enters the expenses data, and also adds comments to explain any unusual entries. Once the data is complete, user C creates charts and graphs to help visualize the data. Throughout the process, track changes is turned on to keep a record of all changes made to the worksheet. If any discrepancies are found, the users can easily go back to the previous version of the worksheet using the track changes feature.

• Importing and exporting data from other sources

Excel is a powerful tool that can import and export data from various sources, making it easier to work with data from different applications. Here are some ways to import and export data in Excel:

1. **Importing Data from a Text File:** To import data from a text file, you can use the "Data" tab in the ribbon and select "From Text/CSV" option. Then browse for the file location and select the file you want to import. You can specify the delimiter, which can be a comma, tab, or semicolon. Excel will then import the data into a new worksheet.

2. **Importing Data from a Database:** To import data from a database, you can use the "Data" tab in the ribbon and select "From Database" option. Then select the database type and enter the server name and credentials. You can then select the table or view from which you want to import data.

3. **Exporting Data to a Text File:** To export data to a text file, you can select the data range you want to export and then use the "Save As" option. Select the file format as "Text (Tab delimited)" or "CSV (Comma delimited)" and save the file.

4. **Exporting Data to a Database:** To export data to a database, you can use the "Data" tab in the ribbon and select "To Database" option. Then select the database type and enter

the server name and credentials. You can then select the table or view to which you want to export data.

5. **Importing Data from Web:** To import data from a web page, you can use the "Data" tab in the ribbon and select "From Web" option. Then enter the URL of the web page from which you want to import data. You can then select the table or view from which you want to import data.

6. **Exporting Data to a Web:** To export data to a web page, you can use the "Publish" option in the "File" tab in the ribbon. Then select the web location where you want to publish the data and select the format in which you want to publish the data.

By using these import and export options, you can easily work with data from various sources and integrate it into your Excel workbook.

Chapter 9:

Tips and Tricks for Excel

• Keyboard shortcuts to save time

Excel offers a wide range of keyboard shortcuts to increase productivity and efficiency. Here are some commonly used keyboard shortcuts in Excel:

1. Ctrl + A: Selects all cells in the current worksheet.
2. Ctrl + C: Copies the selected cells to the clipboard.
3. Ctrl + X: Cuts the selected cells to the clipboard.
4. Ctrl + V: Pastes the contents of the clipboard into the selected cells.
5. Ctrl + Z: Undo the last action.
6. Ctrl + Y: Redo the last undone action.
7. Ctrl + F: Opens the Find and Replace dialog box.
8. Ctrl + H: Opens the Find and Replace dialog box, with Replace tab selected.
9. Ctrl + N: Opens a new workbook.
10. Ctrl + O: Opens an existing workbook.
11. Ctrl + S: Saves the active workbook.
12. Ctrl + P: Opens the Print dialog box.
13. Ctrl + E: Opens the Flash Fill feature.
14. Ctrl + Shift + L: Applies a filter to the selected cells.
15. Ctrl + Shift + P: Opens the Format Cells dialog box.
16. Ctrl + Shift + ~: Formats the selected cells as general.
17. Ctrl + Shift + $: Formats the selected cells as currency.
18. Ctrl + Shift + #: Formats the selected cells as date.
19. Ctrl + Shift + %: Formats the selected cells as percentage.
20. Ctrl + Shift + &: Applies an outline border to the selected cells.
21. Ctrl + Shift + _: Removes the border from the selected cells.
22. Ctrl + Shift + *: Selects the current region around the active cell.
23. Ctrl + Home: Moves the cursor to the beginning of the worksheet.

24. Ctrl + End: Moves the cursor to the last cell with data in the worksheet.
25. F2: Edits the contents of the active cell.
26. F4: Repeats the last action.
27. F11: Creates a chart using the selected data.
28. Alt + =: Automatically sums the selected cells.
29. Alt + Enter: Inserts a new line within a cell.
30. Alt + Tab: Switches between open windows.

These are just a few examples of the many keyboard shortcuts available in Excel. Using keyboard shortcuts can save time and increase productivity when working with large amounts of data.

• Using templates and add-ins

Templates and add-ins are powerful tools in Excel that can help users work more efficiently and effectively. In this section, we will elaborate on using templates and add-ins in Excel with examples.

Templates: Excel templates are pre-designed spreadsheets that users can customize and reuse to suit their specific needs. They can save time and effort by providing pre-formatted designs for a variety of purposes, such as budgeting, tracking, invoicing, and more. Excel templates can be accessed through the File tab, then clicking New, and selecting the desired template.

For example, if you need to create a budget for your business, you can select the "Personal Budget" or "Business Budget" template, and customize it with your own data. This will save you time and effort compared to starting from scratch.

Add-ins: Excel add-ins are supplemental programs that provide additional features and functionality beyond the standard Excel application. They can be used to automate repetitive tasks, perform complex calculations, and enhance data visualization.

There are many Excel add-ins available, both free and paid, which can be downloaded from the Microsoft Store or other online sources. Some popular Excel add-ins include:

1. Power Query: This add-in allows users to easily connect to external data sources, clean and transform data, and create dynamic reports.

2. Solver: This add-in provides a powerful optimization tool for finding optimal solutions to complex problems.

3. Analysis ToolPak: This add-in includes a collection of statistical and financial analysis tools, such as regression analysis, moving averages, and NPV calculations.

4. Kutools for Excel: This add-in provides a wide range of productivity tools, such as merging cells, splitting data, and converting text to date formats.

Using templates and add-ins can help users work more efficiently and effectively in Excel, saving time and effort while providing additional functionality and features.

Power Query

Power Query is a data transformation and cleansing tool available in Excel. It allows you to easily import and transform data from various sources into Excel for analysis and reporting purposes. Power Query can save you a lot of time and effort by automating the process of cleaning and shaping data, which can be very time-consuming if done manually.

Here are some examples of how you can use Power Query in Excel:

Step 1: First thing first. We need to create a connection so that we can pull the data from a text file in Excel. Open an Excel file > Click **Data tab** in Excel ribbon > click **Get Data** dropdown under the **Get & Transform Data** section.

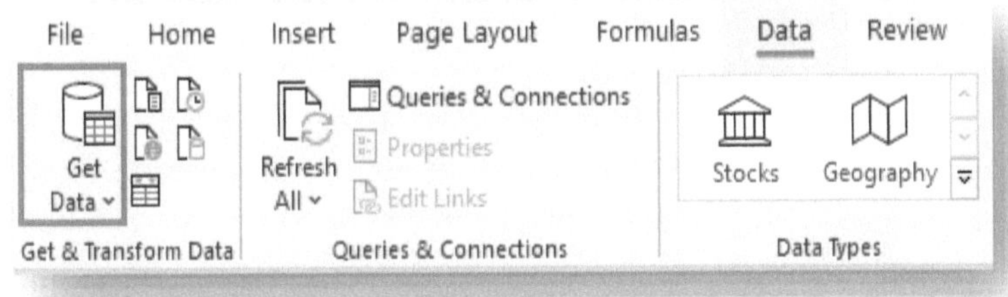

Step 2: As soon as you click on the **Get Data** dropdown, you get several options from where you actually can pull the data. We will navigate towards the option named From Folder, which is under From File dropdown. This option we are using over **From Text/CSV** option because it has more versatility in it than the latter.

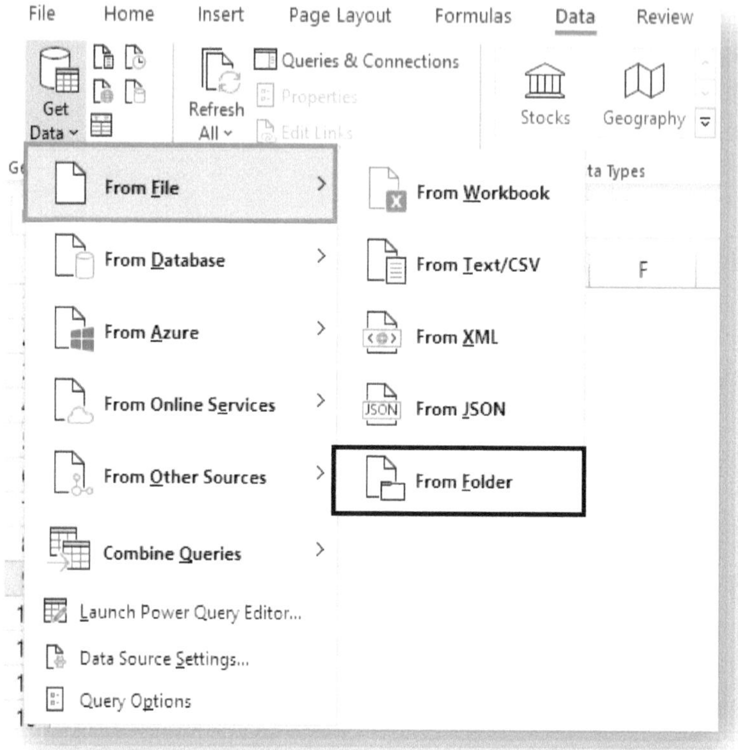

Step 3: As soon as you click on the From Folder option, a new window will pop up. There, you have to browse the path on which the file is located. Click on the **Browse**... button and navigate towards the path where the data file is located.

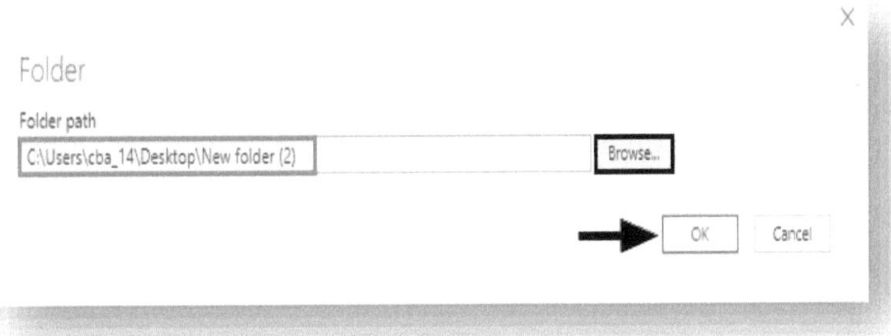

Click on OK once you are done with the path browsing.

NOTE: The path mentioned here in the screenshot is the one where I have located the file. At the time you follow this tutorial, your data file might be stored somewhere else. Browse that path.

Step 4: A new window will open with a list of all files present at the path browsed with different file attributes such as **file name, data type, date modified** and **path** on which the file is located, file extension, etc.

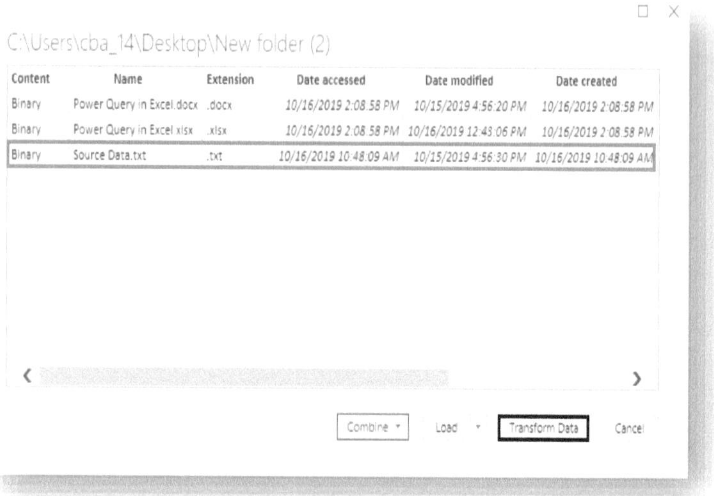

There are 4 more options at the bottom side of this window that reads **Combine, Load, Transform Data, and Cancel.**

Combine allows you to choose between the datasets which you want to combine. However, it doesn't have a separate Edit option, making it less versatile as you can't decide which columns to be combined together.

Load allows you to load the data as a table/Pivot into an Excel sheet irrespective of the actual format of the data under the source file.

Transform Data allows you to transform the source data files. You can add the calculated column, change the format for certain columns, add or remove columns, group columns, etc.

Cancel is a button that cancels all other operations under power Query.

Step 5: Click on the **Transform Data** button and select the file named **Source Data.txt**; you can see the data layout as shown below:

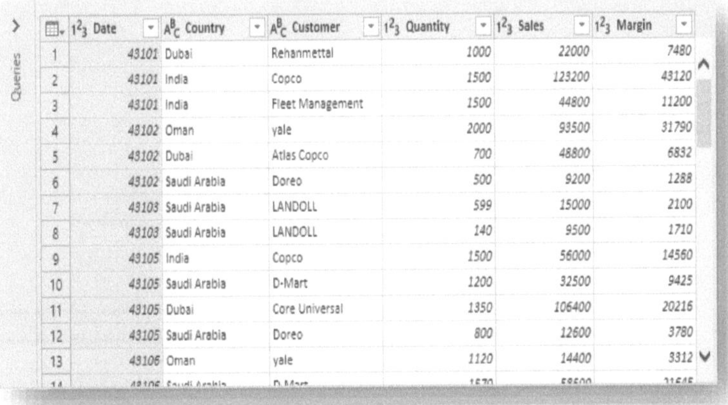

	Date	Country	Customer	Quantity	Sales	Margin
1	43101	Dubai	Rehanmettal	1000	22000	7480
2	43101	India	Copco	1500	123200	43120
3	43101	India	Fleet Management	1500	44800	11200
4	43102	Oman	yale	2000	93500	31790
5	43102	Dubai	Atlas Copco	700	48800	6832
6	43102	Saudi Arabia	Doreo	500	9200	1288
7	43103	Saudi Arabia	LANDOLL	599	15000	2100
8	43103	Saudi Arabia	LANDOLL	140	9500	1710
9	43105	India	Copco	1500	56000	14560
10	43105	Saudi Arabia	D-Mart	1200	32500	9425
11	43105	Dubai	Core Universal	1350	106400	20216
12	43105	Saudi Arabia	Doreo	800	12600	3780
13	43106	Oman	yale	1120	14400	3312

On the upper ribbon, there are several options such as Home, Transform, **Add Column, View.** On the left-hand side of the layout, there is a window for **Query Setting**; we can see all the queries run until here one by one. Please note that each query is a formulated code under Power Query.

Step 6: We now change the data type of the first column to Date. Select the first column named as **Date > Right Click > Change Type navigation bar > Select Date** as an option to represent all the number values as dates for the given column.

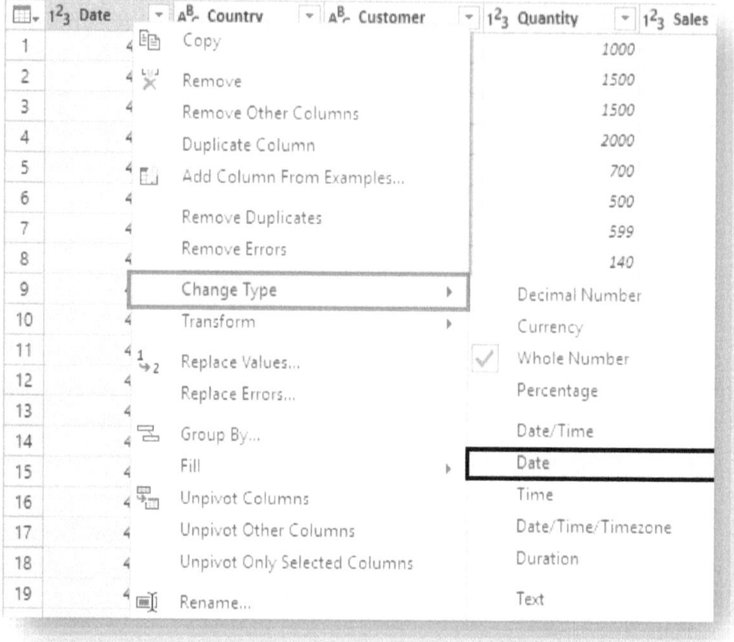

Step 7: As soon as you click on Date, a new window appears named Change Column Type. Click on **Add new step** there to change the format of the column to Date.

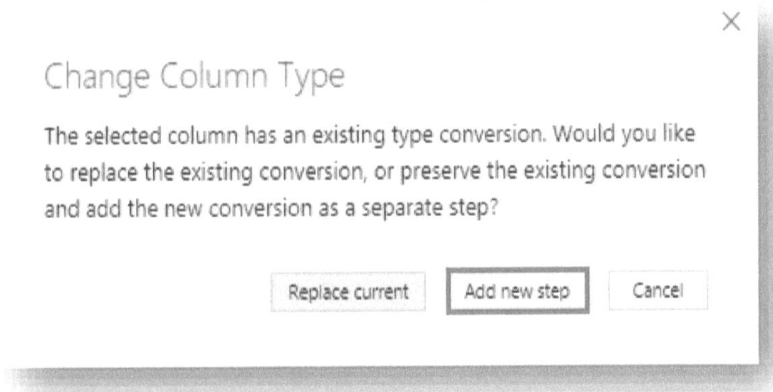

Have a look at the Date column now; it should have changed the format from whole numbers to the Dates.

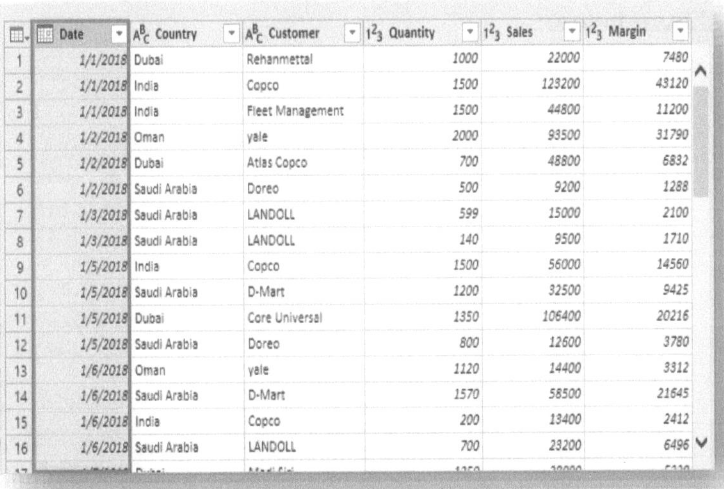

	Date	Country	Customer	Quantity	Sales	Margin
1	1/1/2018	Dubai	Rehanmettal	1000	22000	7480
2	1/1/2018	India	Copco	1500	123200	43120
3	1/1/2018	India	Fleet Management	1500	44800	11200
4	1/2/2018	Oman	yale	2000	93500	31790
5	1/2/2018	Dubai	Atlas Copco	700	48800	6832
6	1/2/2018	Saudi Arabia	Doreo	500	9200	1288
7	1/3/2018	Saudi Arabia	LANDOLL	599	15000	2100
8	1/3/2018	Saudi Arabia	LANDOLL	140	9500	1710
9	1/5/2018	India	Copco	1500	56000	14560
10	1/5/2018	Saudi Arabia	D-Mart	1200	32500	9425
11	1/5/2018	Dubai	Core Universal	1350	106400	20216
12	1/5/2018	Saudi Arabia	Doreo	800	12600	3780
13	1/6/2018	Oman	yale	1120	14400	3312
14	1/6/2018	Saudi Arabia	D-Mart	1570	58500	21645
15	1/6/2018	India	Copco	200	13400	2412
16	1/6/2018	Saudi Arabia	LANDOLL	700	23200	6496

Step 8: We can also add a computed/calculated column under this layout before we load the same. Follow the navigation as **Add Column > Custom Column** under the **General** section. It will allow you to create a new calculated column based on the custom formula.

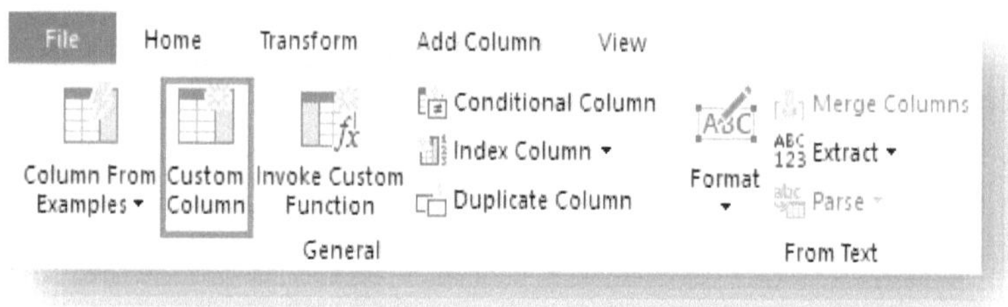

Step 9: Change the name of the column as Margin% and formulate it as Margin/Sales under Custom Column as shown below:

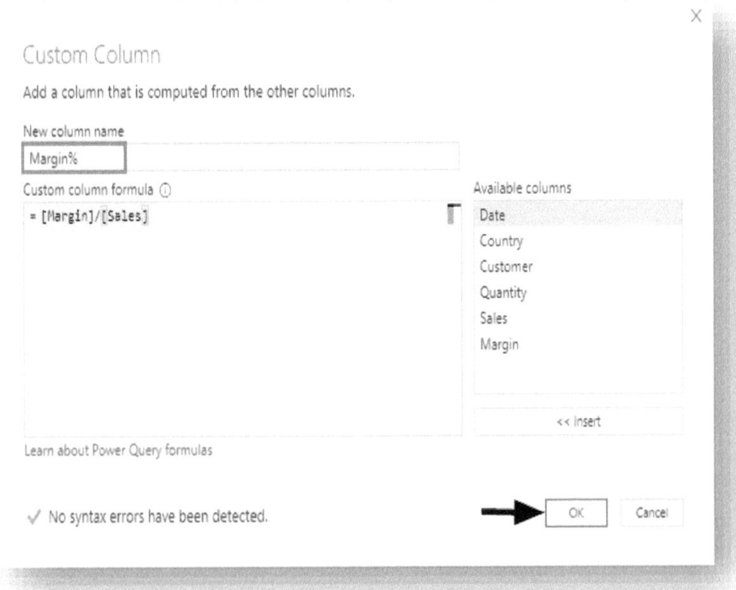

Click the OK button, and you can see the column being added under the layout.

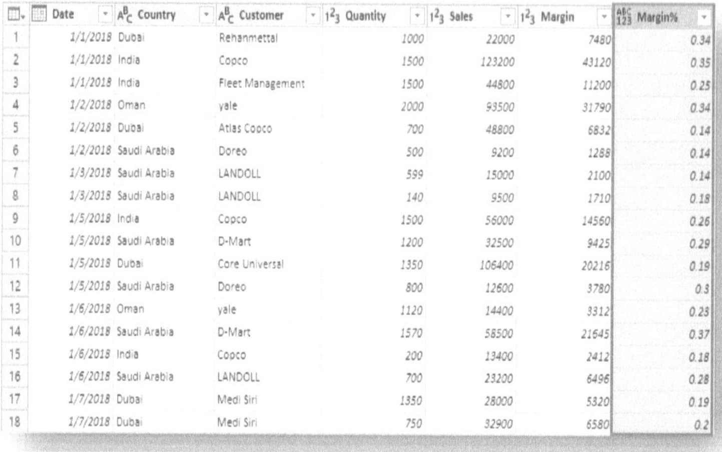

	Date	Country	Customer	Quantity	Sales	Margin	Margin%
1	1/1/2018	Dubai	Rehanmettal	1000	22000	7480	0.34
2	1/1/2018	India	Copco	1500	123200	43120	0.35
3	1/1/2018	India	Fleet Management	1500	44800	11200	0.25
4	1/2/2018	Oman	yale	2000	93500	31790	0.34
5	1/2/2018	Dubai	Atlas Copco	700	48800	6832	0.14
6	1/2/2018	Saudi Arabia	Doreo	500	9200	1288	0.14
7	1/3/2018	Saudi Arabia	LANDOLL	599	15000	2100	0.14
8	1/3/2018	Saudi Arabia	LANDOLL	140	9500	1710	0.18
9	1/5/2018	India	Copco	1500	56000	14560	0.26
10	1/5/2018	Saudi Arabia	D-Mart	1200	32500	9425	0.29
11	1/5/2018	Dubai	Core Universal	1350	106400	20216	0.19
12	1/5/2018	Saudi Arabia	Doreo	800	12600	3780	0.3
13	1/6/2018	Oman	yale	1120	14400	3312	0.23
14	1/6/2018	Saudi Arabia	D-Mart	1570	58500	21645	0.37
15	1/6/2018	India	Copco	200	13400	2412	0.18
16	1/6/2018	Saudi Arabia	LANDOLL	700	23200	6496	0.28
17	1/7/2018	Dubai	Medi Siri	1350	28000	5320	0.19
18	1/7/2018	Dubai	Medi Siri	750	32900	6580	0.2

Step 10: To load this data in Excel, navigate to **Home > Close & Load** navigation bar **> Close & Load To...** option (This option allows you to load the data as Table, PivotTable, PivotTable Chart, etc.)

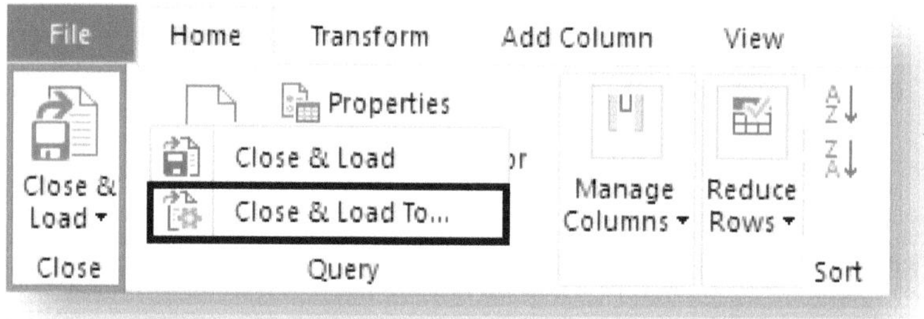

Step 11: Inside the **Import Data** wizard, select the **Table** layout, **Existing Worksheet** and click **OK.**

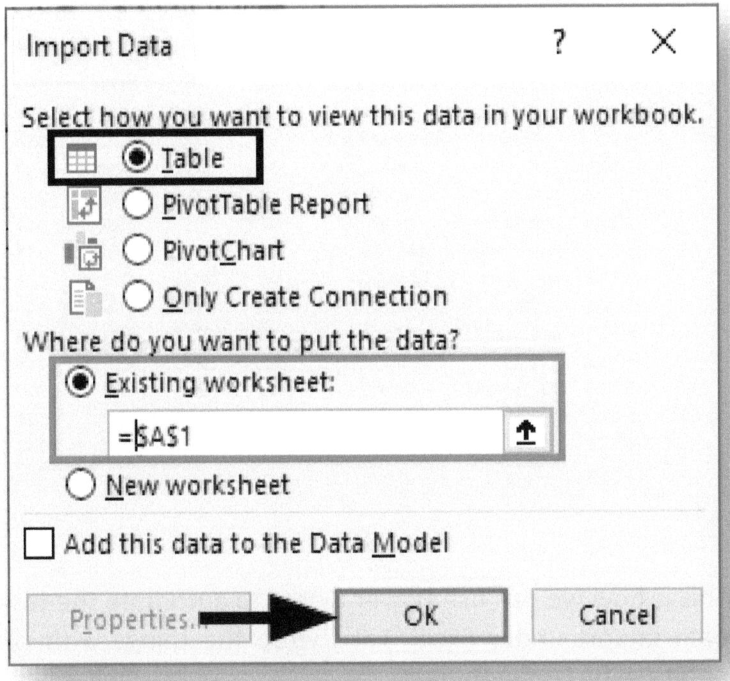

You can see a data table loaded as shown below:

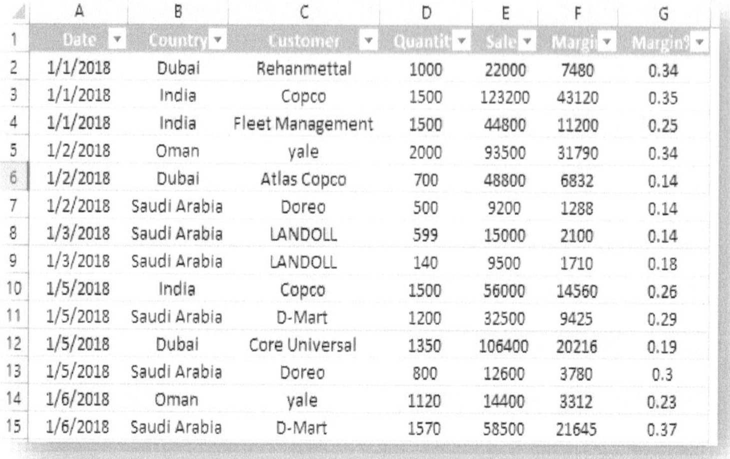

	A	B	C	D	E	F	G
1	Date	Country	Customer	Quantit	Sale	Margi	Margin%
2	1/1/2018	Dubai	Rehanmettal	1000	22000	7480	0.34
3	1/1/2018	India	Copco	1500	123200	43120	0.35
4	1/1/2018	India	Fleet Management	1500	44800	11200	0.25
5	1/2/2018	Oman	yale	2000	93500	31790	0.34
6	1/2/2018	Dubai	Atlas Copco	700	48800	6832	0.14
7	1/2/2018	Saudi Arabia	Doreo	500	9200	1288	0.14
8	1/3/2018	Saudi Arabia	LANDOLL	599	15000	2100	0.14
9	1/3/2018	Saudi Arabia	LANDOLL	140	9500	1710	0.18
10	1/5/2018	India	Copco	1500	56000	14560	0.26
11	1/5/2018	Saudi Arabia	D-Mart	1200	32500	9425	0.29
12	1/5/2018	Dubai	Core Universal	1350	106400	20216	0.19
13	1/5/2018	Saudi Arabia	Doreo	800	12600	3780	0.3
14	1/6/2018	Oman	yale	1120	14400	3312	0.23
15	1/6/2018	Saudi Arabia	D-Mart	1570	58500	21645	0.37

This is how we can use Power Query to automate the task of data import under Excel. Let's wrap the things with some points to be remembered.

Things to Remember

- Power Query is the easiest way to automate the task of data import under Excel. It saves manpower, time as well as reduces human error.
- We can import data from different databases such as SQL Server, Access server, etc., as well as the files such as text, CSV, XML, etc.

Analysis ToolPak

The Analysis ToolPak is an Excel add-in that provides a set of data analysis tools that are not available by default in Excel. These tools can be used to perform various statistical, engineering, and financial analyses, such as regression analysis, t-tests, ANOVA, and moving averages.

To use the Analysis ToolPak, you need to enable it in Excel. Here are the steps:

1. Click on the "File" tab in the ribbon menu and select "Options".

2. In the "Excel Options" window, select "Add-Ins".

3. In the "Manage" dropdown, select "Excel Add-ins" and click "Go".

4. Check the box next to "Analysis ToolPak" and click "OK".

5. The Analysis ToolPak will now be available in the "Data" tab of the ribbon menu.

Here are some examples of how to use the Analysis ToolPak:

1. **Regression analysis:** The Analysis ToolPak can be used to perform regression analysis to determine the relationship between two or more variables. For example, you can use regression analysis to determine the relationship between sales and advertising spend.

2. **Moving averages**: The Analysis ToolPak can be used to calculate moving averages, which are used to smooth out fluctuations in data. For example, you can use moving averages to analyse stock prices over time.

3. **ANOVA:** The Analysis ToolPak can be used to perform ANOVA (Analysis of Variance) to compare the means of multiple groups. For example, you can use ANOVA to determine if there is a significant difference in sales between different regions.

4. **Descriptive statistics:** The Analysis ToolPak can be used to calculate various descriptive statistics, such as mean, median, standard deviation, and variance. For example, you can use descriptive statistics to analyse survey data.

   Overall, the Analysis ToolPak is a powerful tool for data analysis in Excel, and can save you time and effort in performing complex analyses.

1. **Importing data:** Power Query allows you to import data from various sources such as Excel files, CSV files, SQL Server databases, and more. You can easily connect to a data source and load the data into Excel for further analysis.

2. **Transforming data:** Once you have imported the data, you can use Power Query to transform it. You can filter, sort, and reshape the data to make it more useful for your analysis. For example, you can split columns, remove duplicates, and merge tables.

3. **Combining data:** You can use Power Query to combine data from multiple sources into a single table. For example, you can merge data from two different Excel files or combine data from a SQL Server database and a CSV file.

4. **Cleaning data:** Power Query can help you clean and normalize data. For example, you can remove extra spaces, convert data types, and fill in missing values.

5. **Automating data refresh:** You can set up Power Query to automatically refresh your data when you open your Excel file or on a specific schedule. This ensures that your data is always up to date.

Overall, Power Query is a powerful tool that can save you time and effort in cleaning and transforming data in Excel.

Solver

Solver is an add-in tool in Excel that can be used to find an optimal solution for a problem, given certain constraints and variables. It is particularly useful for problems involving optimization, such as maximizing profits or minimizing costs.

Here are some examples of how Solver can be used in Excel:

Maximizing profits: Suppose a company produces two types of products, A and B, using two different machines, X and Y. The profit per unit for each product is as follows:

- Product A: $10 (machine X), $8 (machine Y)

- Product B: $12 (machine X), $6 (machine Y)

The company has a limited number of hours available on each machine per week:

- Machine X: 80 hours
- Machine Y: 60 hours

The company wants to know how many units of each product to produce to maximize profits, given these constraints.

To use Solver for this problem, you would set up a spreadsheet with the profit per unit for each product and machine, and the hours available on each machine. You would then use Solver to find the maximum profit by changing the number of units produced for each product subject to the constraints of available machine hours.

Minimizing costs: Suppose a company wants to produce a certain number of products at the lowest possible cost. The cost per unit for each raw material and the production time per unit are as follows:

- Raw material A: $5 per unit
- Raw material B: $8 per unit
- Production time: 2 hours per unit

The company has a limited budget for raw materials and a limited number of production hours available:

- Budget for raw materials: $1000
- Production hours available: 100

The company wants to know how many units to produce of each product to minimize costs, given these constraints.

To use Solver for this problem, you would set up a spreadsheet with the cost per unit for each raw material and the production time per unit, and the budget for raw materials and production hours available. You would then use Solver to find the minimum cost by changing the number of units produced for each product subject to the constraints of available budget and production hours.

In both examples, Solver can be used to find an optimal solution by changing the values of certain cells (the number of units produced for each product) subject to certain constraints (the available machine hours, raw material budget, and production hours). Solver then calculates the maximum or minimum value of a certain cell (the profit or cost per unit) based on the changing cells and constraints.

Kutools

Kutools for Excel is an add-in software that enhances the functionality of Microsoft Excel. It provides a range of useful features and tools to simplify complex tasks in Excel. Some of the key features of Kutools include:

1. **Combine Rows and Columns:** This tool allows you to quickly combine multiple rows or columns into one.

2. **Split Cells:** With this tool, you can split a cell into multiple cells based on a delimiter or fixed width.

3. **Insert Multiple Rows and Columns:** This feature enables you to insert multiple rows or columns at once.

4. **Batch Convert:** This tool enables you to batch convert Excel files to other formats such as PDF, CSV, and more.

5. **Super Filter**: This tool provides advanced filtering options for your data.

6. **Range Converter:** With this tool, you can quickly convert a range of cells from one type to another, such as text to number or vice versa.

7. **Duplicate Finder:** This tool helps you find and remove duplicates in your data.

8. **Export Range as File:** This tool allows you to export a selected range of cells as a separate file.

9. **Navigation Pane:** This feature provides a handy navigation pane that makes it easier to navigate large Excel spreadsheets.

10. **Insert Bullet:** With this tool, you can quickly insert bullet points into your worksheet.

Kutools for Excel is a paid software, but it offers a free trial version that allows you to try out some of its features. Overall, Kutools can be a valuable addition to your Excel toolkit, especially if you frequently work with large or complex spreadsheets.

• Troubleshooting common issues in Excel

Excel is a powerful tool that can help users perform complex calculations and data analysis with ease. However, like any software, Excel can sometimes encounter issues that may require troubleshooting. In this section, we will discuss some common issues that users may encounter in Excel and how to troubleshoot them.

1. **Excel crashes or freezes:** One common issue with Excel is that it can crash or freeze unexpectedly. This can happen for a variety of reasons, including running too many calculations, having too many open workbooks, or encountering errors in formulas. To troubleshoot this issue, you can try closing any unnecessary workbooks, reducing the number of calculations or complex formulas, or disabling any add-ins that may be causing conflicts. You can also try repairing or reinstalling Excel to fix any corrupted files.

2. **Unable to open a file:** This can happen due to various reasons such as a corrupted file, incorrect file extension, or outdated software. To troubleshoot this issue, try opening the file in another version of Excel or using an online file converter to change the file format.

3. **Errors in formulas:** Excel formulas can sometimes produce errors, such as #DIV/0!, #VALUE!, or #NAME?. These errors can occur if the formula references a cell that contains an

error, if the formula is incomplete or contains syntax errors, or if the formula is referencing data that has been deleted or moved. To troubleshoot formula errors, you can try checking the syntax of the formula, making sure that all cell references are valid, or using the Trace Error tool to identify the source of the error.

4. **Printing issues:** Excel may encounter issues while printing, such as distorted or incomplete printouts. One way to troubleshoot this issue is to check the print settings and adjust them accordingly. Another way is to check the printer settings and ensure that the printer driver is up to date.

5. **Data entry errors:** Users may sometimes make errors while entering data into Excel, such as incorrect formatting, misspelled words, or wrong calculations. One way to troubleshoot this issue is to use the data validation feature in Excel to ensure that the data entered is correct. Another way is to use the spell-check feature to correct any spelling errors.

6. **Security warnings:** Excel may display security warnings when opening a file that contains macros or external data sources. One way to troubleshoot this issue is to enable macro security settings and ensure that external data sources are trusted.

7. **Incorrect data entry:** Another common issue in Excel is incorrect data entry, such as misspelled words, incorrect dates, or incorrect formatting. To troubleshoot this issue, you can use data validation to limit the types of data that can be entered into a cell, or use formatting tools to highlight incorrect or inconsistent data. You can also use Excel's text

functions to clean up or format data that has been entered incorrectly.

8. **Printing issues:** Excel can sometimes encounter issues when printing, such as printing blank pages, printing only part of a worksheet, or printing with incorrect margins or page breaks. To troubleshoot printing issues, you can try adjusting the page margins and page breaks, checking the printer settings and drivers, or saving the workbook as a PDF and printing from the PDF file.

9. **Slow performance:** Excel can become slow or unresponsive if the workbook is too large, if there are too many calculations or complex formulas, or if the computer is low on memory or processing power. To troubleshoot slow performance issues, you can try closing any unnecessary workbooks, reducing the size and complexity of the workbook, or adding more memory or processing power to the computer.

In conclusion, these are some common issues that users may encounter in Excel and how to troubleshoot them. By understanding these issues and following the recommended troubleshooting steps, users can avoid potential roadblocks and work more efficiently in Excel.

• Best practices for organizing and managing data

Sure, here are some more specific examples of best practices for organizing and managing data in Excel:

1. **Use tables:** Tables are a great way to organize and manage data in Excel. They provide structure to your data, making it easier to sort and filter, and enable you to analyse your data more efficiently. For example, if you have a list of customers and their orders, you can create a table that includes columns for customer name, order date, order amount, and so on. This makes it easier to track orders over time and to identify which customers are the most profitable.

2. **Use named ranges:** Named ranges allow you to refer to specific cells or ranges of cells by name rather than by their cell reference. This makes it easier to write formulas and to navigate large worksheets. For example, if you have a list of expenses and you want to calculate the total amount for a particular category, you can create a named range for the category column and then reference that name in your formula.

3. **Keep data on one sheet:** Keeping all related data on one sheet is a best practice because it makes it easier to find and manage your data. For example, if you have a workbook that contains multiple sheets for different departments, you can create a summary sheet that pulls data from all of the other sheets. This way, you can see all of the data in one place without having to navigate between different sheets.

4. **Use data validation:** Data validation is a best practice because it helps ensure that your data is accurate and consistent. For example, if you have a column for email addresses, you can use data validation to ensure that each entry is a valid email address. This helps prevent errors and makes it easier to filter and sort your data.

5. **Use conditional formatting:** Conditional formatting is a best practice because it allows you to visually highlight important data and identify trends or patterns. For example, if you have a list of sales data, you can use conditional formatting to highlight the top-selling products or to create a colour scale that shows which products are performing well and which are not.

6. **Use filters:** Filters are a best practice because they allow you to quickly and easily sort and analyse your data. For example, if you have a list of sales data, you can use filters to view sales by product, by region, or by time period. This makes it easier to identify trends and to analyse your data more efficiently.

7. **Use pivot tables:** Pivot tables are a best practice because they allow you to summarize and analyse large amounts of data quickly and easily. For example, if you have a list of sales data, you can use a pivot table to summarize sales by product, by region, or by time period. This makes it easier to identify trends and to analyse your data more efficiently.

8. **Keep data clean:** Keeping your data clean is a best practice because it helps prevent errors and ensures that your data is consistent and accurate. For example, if you have a list of customer names, you can use Excel's text functions to

remove any unnecessary characters or spaces. This makes it easier to sort and filter your data and reduces the risk of errors.

9. **Protect your data:** Protecting your data is a best practice because it helps prevent unauthorized changes or deletions to your data. For example, if you have a workbook that contains sensitive financial data, you can use Excel's password protection feature to prevent unauthorized access to the workbook. This helps ensure that your data is secure and that only authorized users have access to it.

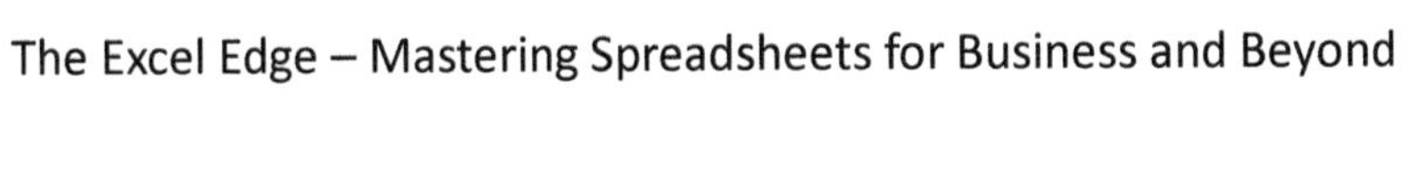

Chapter 10:

Excel for Business

• Using Excel for financial analysis

Financial analysis is a critical component of financial decision-making, and Excel is a powerful tool that can help you perform various financial analysis tasks. Here are some examples of how to use Excel for financial analysis:

1. **Financial statement analysis:** Excel can be used to analyse financial statements such as the income statement, balance sheet, and cash flow statement. You can use Excel's built-in functions to calculate various financial ratios such as profitability ratios, liquidity ratios, and solvency ratios. For example, you can use the formula "=Net Profit / Total Revenue" to calculate the net profit margin ratio.

2. **Budgeting and forecasting:** Excel is also useful for creating budgets and forecasting future financial performance. You can use Excel's built-in functions to create budgets and forecasts based on historical data. For example, you can use the formula "=GROWTH(Revenue)" to forecast future revenue based on historical revenue data.

3. **Sensitivity analysis:** Excel is great for performing sensitivity analysis, which involves analysing how changes in certain variables affect financial outcomes. For example, you can use Excel to create a sensitivity analysis table that shows how changes in interest rates or other variables affect the net present value (NPV) of an investment.

4. **Investment analysis:** Excel can also be used to perform investment analysis, which involves analysing the financial

viability of potential investments. For example, you can use Excel to calculate the NPV, internal rate of return (IRR), and payback period of an investment.

5. **Valuation analysis:** Excel is a powerful tool for performing valuation analysis, which involves determining the intrinsic value of a company or asset. You can use Excel to calculate various valuation metrics such as discounted cash flow (DCF) and price-to-earnings (P/E) ratios. For example, you can use the formula "=NPV(discount rate, cash flows)" to calculate the present value of future cash flows in a DCF analysis.

6. **Portfolio analysis:** Excel can be used to analyse investment portfolios, such as stocks and bonds. You can use Excel to calculate various portfolio metrics such as the average return, standard deviation, and beta. For example, you can use the formula "=AVERAGE(Returns)" to calculate the average return of a portfolio.

7. **Risk analysis:** Excel is also useful for performing risk analysis, which involves analysing the potential risks and rewards of various financial decisions. You can use Excel to calculate various risk metrics such as the value at risk (VaR) and the expected shortfall (ES). For example, you can use the formula "=NORM.INV(probability, mean, standard deviation)" to calculate the VaR of a portfolio.

In conclusion, Excel is a powerful tool for financial analysis, and it can be used for a wide range of financial analysis tasks. Whether you are analysing financial statements, creating budgets and forecasts, performing sensitivity analysis, or conducting investment and valuation analysis, Excel can help you make informed financial decisions and provide insights into your financial data.

• Creating and managing budgets

Creating and managing budgets in Excel is an excellent way to track your expenses, manage your finances, and achieve your financial goals. Here are some practical steps and examples to guide you in creating and managing budgets in Excel.

1. **Identify your budget categories** Start by identifying your budget categories. These categories will vary depending on your lifestyle, expenses, and financial goals. Common budget categories include rent/mortgage, transportation, food, utilities, entertainment, insurance, and savings.
2. **Create a budget template** Once you have identified your budget categories, create a budget template in Excel. You can create a template from scratch or use one of the pre-built templates available in Excel.

   Here are some examples of budget templates in Excel:

1. **Basic budget template:** This template includes essential categories such as housing, transportation, food, and entertainment, along with spaces to input your budgeted amounts and actual expenses.

2. **Detailed budget template:** This template includes more detailed categories such as rent/mortgage, utilities, groceries, dining out, clothing, and personal care, along with spaces to input your budgeted amounts and actual expenses.

3. **Monthly budget template:** This template allows you to track your expenses on a monthly basis. It includes spaces to input your budgeted amounts and actual expenses for each month, along with a summary of your expenses for the year.

4. **Family budget template:** This template is designed for families and includes categories such as childcare, education, and medical expenses, along with spaces to input your budgeted amounts and actual expenses.

5. **Debt reduction template:** This template is designed to help you track your debt repayment progress. It includes spaces to input your debt balances, interest rates, and monthly payments, along with a summary of your progress.

6. **Rolling budget template:** This template allows you to track your budget over multiple months and includes spaces to input your budgeted amounts and actual expenses for each month, along with a running total for the year.

7. **Budget analysis template:** This template includes charts and graphs to help you analyse your budget data and identify areas where you may need to make adjustments.

To create a budget template from scratch, start by opening a new workbook in Excel. Then, create a table with the following columns: Category, Budgeted Amount, Actual Amount, and Variance. Enter your budget categories in the Category column and your budgeted amounts in the Budgeted Amount column. You can leave the Actual Amount and Variance columns blank for now.

1. **Determine your budget categories:** Start by determining the different categories you want to include in your budget, such as housing, transportation, food, entertainment, etc.

2. **Create a budget template:** Create a budget template in Excel that includes the categories you identified in step 1, along with spaces to input your actual expenses and compare them to your budgeted amounts.

3. **Input your budgeted amounts:** Input the budgeted amounts for each category in the appropriate cells of the budget template. For example, if you budgeted $500 per month for food, input "500" in the cell next to the "Food" category.

4. **Input your actual expenses:** Input your actual expenses for each category in the appropriate cells of the budget template. For example, if you spent $550 on food during a particular month, input "550" in the cell next to the "Food" category.

5. **Calculate the variance:** Calculate the variance between your actual expenses and your budgeted amounts by subtracting the budgeted amount from the actual expense amount. For example, if you budgeted $500 for food and spent $550, the variance would be -$50.

6. **Analyse the results:** Analyse the results of your budget by looking at the variances between your actual expenses and your budgeted amounts. If you are consistently overspending in a particular category, you may need to adjust your budgeted amount or look for ways to reduce your expenses.

7. **Make adjustments:** Make adjustments to your budget as needed based on your actual expenses and your financial goals. For example, if you consistently overspend on entertainment, you may need to reduce your budgeted amount or look for ways to save money in that category.

In conclusion, creating and managing budgets in Excel is a useful tool for managing your finances and achieving your financial goals. By following these practical steps and using one of the templates mentioned above, you can easily create a budget and track your expenses to ensure you stay within your financial means.

• Forecasting sales and expenses

Forecasting sales and expenses is a critical component of any business plan. It allows you to project your expected income and expenses, which in turn helps you make informed decisions regarding budgeting, investment, and growth strategies. In this section, we will explore how to use Excel to forecast sales and expenses.

1. **Gather historical data** The first step in forecasting sales and expenses is to gather historical data. You will need to collect information about your past sales, expenses, and any other relevant factors that may impact your future income and expenses. This can include factors such as economic trends, industry changes, and customer behaviour.

2. **Determine your forecasting period** Next, determine the period for which you want to forecast your sales and expenses. This could be a week, a month, a quarter, or a year, depending on your business needs.

3. **Create a forecast worksheet** in Excel Create a new worksheet in Excel, and create columns to input your data. Your worksheet should include the following columns:

- **Date:** The date of the forecast period.

- **Sales:** The total sales expected for the period.

- **Cost of Goods Sold (COGS):** The cost of producing the goods sold.

- **Gross Profit:** The difference between sales and COGS.
- **Operating Expenses:** The expected expenses to run the business.
- **Net Income:** The difference between gross profit and operating expenses.

4. **Input historical data** Input the historical data you collected into the appropriate columns. This data will provide a baseline for your forecast.
5. **Identify trends Analyse** the historical data to identify trends that may impact your future sales and expenses. For example, if you notice a seasonal pattern in your sales, you may need to adjust your forecast accordingly.
6. **Forecast sales** Use a sales forecasting method to project your expected sales for the forecast period. There are several methods you can use, including:

- **Trend analysis:** This method involves analysing historical data to identify trends and projecting future sales based on those trends.
- **Regression analysis:** This method involves using statistical techniques to analyse historical data and identify the relationships between different factors that impact sales, such as advertising spend and sales volume.
- **Time-series analysis:** This method involves analysing historical data to identify seasonal patterns and other trends

that impact sales and projecting future sales based on those trends.

7. **Forecast expenses** Use a similar method to forecast your expected expenses for the forecast period. Consider factors such as inflation, changes in pricing, and increases or decreases in operational expenses.

8. **Create a forecast summary** Once you have input your sales and expenses forecasts, create a summary of your projected income statement for the forecast period. This summary should include the following:

- Total Sales
- Cost of Goods Sold (COGS)
- Gross Profit
- Operating Expenses
- Net Income

9. **Review and adjust** Review your forecast and adjust it based on any new information or changes in your business or industry. For example, if you receive new market research that indicates a potential increase in demand for your product, adjust your sales forecast accordingly.

   Here is an example of a sales and expense forecasting worksheet in Excel:

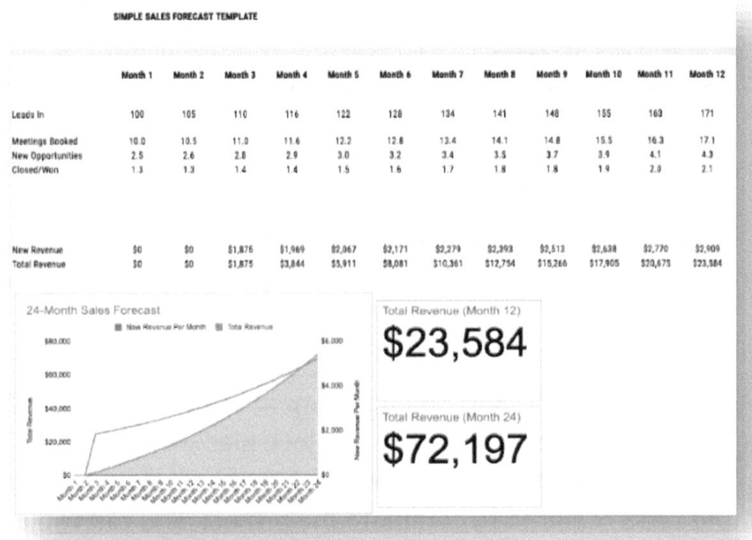

SIMPLE SALES FORECAST TEMPLATE

	Month 1	Month 2	Month 3	Month 4	Month 5	Month 6	Month 7	Month 8	Month 9	Month 10	Month 11	Month 12
Leads In	100	105	110	116	122	128	134	141	148	155	163	171
Meetings Booked	10.0	10.5	11.0	11.6	12.2	12.8	13.4	14.1	14.8	15.5	16.3	17.1
New Opportunities	2.5	2.6	2.8	2.9	3.0	3.2	3.4	3.5	3.7	3.9	4.1	4.3
Closed/Won	1.3	1.3	1.4	1.4	1.5	1.6	1.7	1.8	1.8	1.9	2.0	2.1
New Revenue	$0	$0	$1,875	$1,969	$2,067	$2,171	$2,279	$2,393	$2,513	$2,638	$2,770	$2,909
Total Revenue	$0	$0	$1,875	$3,844	$5,911	$8,081	$10,361	$12,754	$15,266	$17,905	$20,675	$23,584

In conclusion, forecasting sales and expenses is a crucial part of running a successful business. By gathering historical data, identifying trends, and using appropriate forecasting methods, you can create accurate forecasts to help guide your business decisions. Using Excel to create and manage your forecasting data can be an efficient and effective way to make informed financial decisions for your business.

• Using Excel for project management and tracking

Using Excel for project management and tracking is a popular choice for businesses of all sizes. Excel offers a variety of tools and features that can help you plan, track, and manage your projects more effectively. In this section, we will explore how to use Excel for project management and tracking with examples.

1. **Create a project plan** The first step in using Excel for project management is to create a project plan. This plan should outline the scope of the project, the timeline, the budget, and the tasks required to complete the project. You can use Excel to create a project plan by setting up a Gantt chart, which is a visual representation of the project timeline and tasks.

2. **Create a project schedule** Once you have created a project plan, you can use Excel to create a project schedule. This schedule should include the start and end dates for each task, as well as the dependencies between tasks. You can use Excel's conditional formatting tools to highlight tasks that are overdue or behind schedule.

3. **Track project progress** As you work on your project, you can use Excel to track your progress. One way to do this is by updating your Gantt chart and project schedule with the actual start and end dates for each task. You can also use Excel's status reporting tools to create visual reports that show the progress of each task.

4. **Manage project resources** Excel can also be used to manage project resources, such as personnel and materials. You can create a resource allocation table in Excel that shows the availability of each resource and the tasks that each resource is assigned to. This can help you ensure that you have the necessary resources to complete your project on time and within budget.

5. **Create project budget and cost tracking** Excel is also useful for creating and tracking project budgets and costs. You can create a budget worksheet in Excel that includes estimates for each expense category, as well as the actual costs for each category. You can also use Excel to track expenses, such as materials, labour, and equipment, as they occur.

6. **Analyse project performance** Once your project is complete, you can use Excel to analyse its performance. You can create a post-project analysis worksheet in Excel that includes metrics such as the project's actual cost, its actual duration, and the variance between the actual and estimated costs and durations. This can help you identify areas where you can improve your project management processes in the future.

   Here is an example of a project tracking template in Excel:

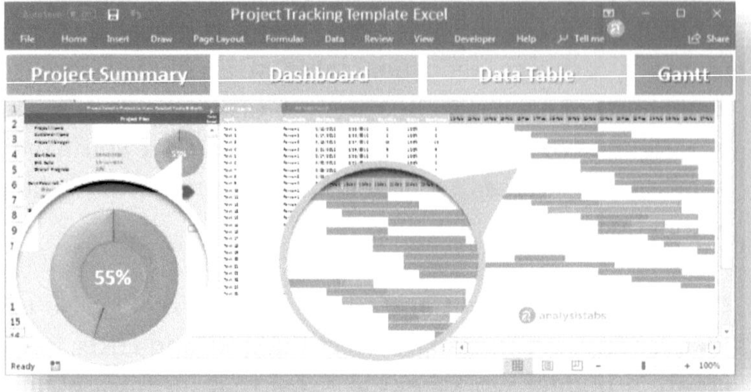

In conclusion, using Excel for project management and tracking can help you plan, track, and manage your projects more effectively. By creating a project plan, schedule, and budget in Excel, and using its reporting and analysis tools, you can ensure that your projects are completed on time, within budget, and to your satisfaction.

www.ingramcontent.com/pod-product-compliance
Ingram Content Group UK Ltd.
Pitfield, Milton Keynes, MK11 3LW, UK
UKHW041639190726
13854UKWH00006B/2582